Praise for *Develop*

"Essential. Ted Fleming's *Develop* is a powerful new resource, and his seven tools provide a powerful framework guiding individuals from early career to seasoned executive. The true value in this book lies in the practical application of how to leverage current experience for future success and career satisfaction."

—Phil Guido, general manager, IBM Services Cloud Transformation

"*Develop* is the rare book that will help each reader tap into their unique talents, while also acknowledging their unique challenges, as they forge a path toward personal success. A must read for anyone beginning their career."

—Elease Wright, vice chair of the National Academy of Human Resources

"In *Develop*, Ted Fleming has provided indispensable knowledge and practical tips to help you develop an effective game plan to advance your career. The book provides an essential foundation to building a bridge to your future and one could not ask for a better tutorial on how you can envision it. The section on Special Circumstances is one of the best guides to help women and people of color understand how to negotiate the unique obstacles they may encounter as they ascend to senior level positions. *Develop* offers valuable counsel on every page."

—Ron Williams, chairman and CEO of RW2 Enterprises, LLC, and author of *Learning to Lead*

"If you hate networking, you'll love *Develop*. If you're searching for a more fulfilling career, you'll discover how to find one. Fleming takes the angst out of making a career or job change with his seven tools grounded in research and deep experience."

—Margaret H. Greenberg, MAPP, executive coach and author of *Profit from the Positive*

"In career development, knowing what you want to do is important, but it's not enough. Ted Fleming's book *Develop* provides you with a road map for acquiring the skills, experience and education you'll need to succeed and fulfill your professional potential."

—Kathy McAfee, "America's Marketing Motivator" and author of *Stop Global Boring*

DEVELOP

DEVELOP

7 PRACTICAL TOOLS TO TAKE CHARGE OF YOUR CAREER

TED FLEMING

HEAD OF TALENT DEVELOPMENT FOR

A FORTUNE 10 COMPANY

BenBella Books, Inc.
Dallas, TX

BenBella

BenBella Books, Inc.
10440 N. Central Expressway, Suite 800
Dallas, TX 75231
www.benbellabooks.com
Send feedback to feedback@benbellabooks.com

BenBella is a federally registered trademark.

Printed in the United States of America
10 9 8 7 6 5 4 3 2 1

Library of Congress Cataloging-in-Publication Data:
Names: Fleming, Ted, author.
Title: Develop : 7 practical tools to take charge of your career / Ted Fleming.
Description: Dallas : BenBella Books, 2020. | Includes bibliographical references
Identifiers: LCCN 2020016838 (print) | LCCN 2020016839 (ebook) |
    ISBN 9781950665358 (hardback) | ISBN 9781950665525 (ebook)
Subjects: LCSH: Career development. | Vocational guidance.
Classification: LCC HF5381 .F596 2020 (print) | LCC HF5381 (ebook) | DDC
    650.1—dc23
LC record available at https://lccn.loc.gov/2020016838
LC ebook record available at https://lccn.loc.gov/2020016839

Editing by Claire Schulz
Copyediting by Scott Calamar
Proofreading by Lisa Story
    and James Fraleigh
Text design by Publishers' Design and
    Production Services, Inc.

Text composition by Katie Hollister
Indexing by WordCo Indexing Services, Inc.
Cover design by Kara Klontz
Printed by Lake Book Manufacturing

Distributed to the trade by Two Rivers Distribution, an Ingram brand
www.tworiversdistribution.com

Special discounts for bulk sales are available.
Please contact bulkorders@benbellabooks.com.

To Kathryn, for always supporting me.
To Gus (Dad) Young, Marty Fein, and Ruth Bruck,
who gave me guidance and inspired me to be a good person. I miss them.

Contents

INTRODUCTION

Why I Wrote This Book

If you are reading this book, chances are you are ready for a change. You might like your job or company, but you want to get ahead and don't know what to do next. Maybe it has been a long time since you've had to look for a job and need a road map. Or maybe you're unhappy and you're searching for the path to a more rewarding job and career. If that's you, you're not alone. According to the 2019 "Mind the Workplace" report (released by Mental Health America and the Faas Foundation), more than half of Americans are dissatisfied at work and actively hunting for a new job. (And 41 percent of them look for different employment several times a week!) This is just one of many studies I could cite that document people's frustration with their jobs.

But will getting a new job make them truly happy? Not likely. Few people know exactly what they want in a job or how to get it. We often need help finding our way. Without a road map, we can feel overwhelmed and powerless to change our situation. This leads to frustration and isolation that results in a disengaged and uninspired workforce. When I give workshops and seminars, I prompt the audience, "Raise your hand if you've worked at the same company for the last three years." Then I follow that with, "Keep your hand up if you've had the same job for those three years."

When the attendees look around the room, they notice that almost everyone's hand is still raised. This should be your first insight. Despite all the studies and employee survey results on job satisfaction (or lack thereof), the majority of people work at the same company, in the same role, year after year. So, any book on how to master the skills needed to perform well in your current role—or to get the experience you need to get promoted in the future—should focus on how to excel in your current role as well as how to look for a new job. Growing within your current role can take just as much effort as applying for a new job, and yet, not many books address it.

I've worked with thousands of people over many years in the areas of career and leadership development. I see firsthand the fear, frustration, and struggle they experience as they try to navigate their organizations. Most people do not take a systematic approach to development, which results in stalled progression and working in unfulfilling jobs. Simply put, they struggle to communicate what they want, don't understand the needs of their managers and employers, don't network effectively, haven't crafted a powerful image, or don't know how to circumvent barriers others place in their way.

Develop: 7 Practical Tools for Taking Charge of Your Career has grown out of twenty-plus years of experience as a leadership-development practitioner and researcher working with colleagues across numerous industries. It shares simple, relevant, and easy-to-apply guidance for finding the right job or growing in an existing job. Alongside the seven tools I've created for my clients and mentees, *Develop* also shares what I've found to be the most useful theories and exercises from textbooks and other career guides. These are actionable tools and techniques that you can apply systematically to achieve your career goals and higher levels of job satisfaction.

How did I come to create this tool kit? A little about my personal background may be in order.

I've had an interesting career! I've worked as a substitute teacher, banker, strategist, consultant, and human resources professional. My industry experiences include education, financial services, media and entertainment, not-for-profit economic development, and healthcare.

Although I've worked across different industries in different capacities, one consistent role stands out: that of advisor. Early in my career I advised students trying to master English and reading skills. I didn't know it at the time, but good teachers are experts at understanding people at an individual level. We are all individuals, motivated by different things. I learned how to tailor my approach, examples, and messages so each student could grasp a concept. A story might work for one person, while an exercise or some homework would work for others. Career development, like classroom learning, is personal.

Later, as a banker, I advised leaders on merger and acquisition strategies and financial matters. Banking taught me how to analyze businesses and the people who run them. I learned that it is not enough to have a good business idea: you also need the leadership team, capital, and infrastructure to make a venture successful. In career development, knowing what you want to do is important, but it's not enough. You need a road map for acquiring the skills, experiences, and education it takes to succeed.

After that, I worked in enterprise strategy for two large organizations and served as the chief of staff to a chief executive officer and a chief operating officer. Those experiences taught me how to advise the most senior leaders in an organization—how to articulate and execute their visions. I translated their ideas into actionable strategies, project plans, and metrics to help guide one organization through a rapid growth period, and another organization through a turnaround. Working with C-suite executives requires great influencing skills, the ability to tell truth to power, and organizational savvy to navigate political waters. (I will share insights for how you can navigate career transitions, better articulate how you can add value to an organization, and use networking to manage politics.)

Then something happened that changed my career focus and integrated all of my past experiences.

In 2010, I was the executive director of strategy for Aetna. I visited a company in Cambridge, Massachusetts, that was working to improve the consumer experience for our medical members. It looked like a typical high-tech start-up scene you'd see in a movie: small groups of people brainstorming, walls covered with drawings and notes, wireframes of websites in a large open area. A young consultant walked up to me and asked, "Are you Ted Fleming? You have a phone call from Mark Bertolini's office."

He was the president of the company, so I said I should probably take that call. When I got on the phone, I heard, "Congratulations, you are moving to HR; come back to Hartford." I'd been appointed vice president of talent management, responsible for talent acquisition, talent development, change management, and organizational consulting. Over the next two years I got a crash course on how to attract, retain, develop, and reward people. I presented each week to our executive committee . . . or, more accurately, I was in the hot seat answering questions on how we were developing the talent we needed to achieve our growth goals. It was a seven-day-a-week job that was one of the best learning experiences of my career. A true baptism by fire as I had not worked in human resources previously.

Over those two years, I led the design and implementation of a new HR operating model to improve the efficiency and effectiveness of how we hired new talent. We cut the time to fill executive-level jobs from seven weeks to six weeks. We also designed and implemented new leadership development programs for regional general managers.

It was hard work, but after sixteen months I was feeling comfortable in my new role. Then the phone rang again. I was called up to our eighth-floor executive offices to see now CEO Mark Bertolini. It was a beautiful office with antique furniture and a working fireplace, and best of all, Lucky, Mark's dog, was there to greet me. A golden retriever, Lucky was a celebrity with an employee badge. As I sat down on the couch, Lucky sat beside me and I petted her as Mark told me my job was about to change. He said, "I've been waiting two years for a corporate university, but nothing has happened. You are going to create Aetna University." I asked if I had one or two years to create the program. He laughed and said, "You have ninety days."

That day I ordered three books on creating corporate universities, picked them up at my local bookstore, and read them all over the weekend. I then spoke to several people who created or ran corporate universities for advice. I had officially moved from the strategy of organizations to the strategy of people—from advising professionals and executives to guiding the careers of the entire organization.

Now, I started this research on success long before Mark Bertolini charged me with creating Aetna University. When I was a banker, I won an award as one of the top salespeople in the company. After the announcement, several people came up to me and said, "I didn't think you did anything." I did not act like other bankers, so they couldn't understand how I was successful. Most of my peers pored over financial statements, monitored stock market fluctuations, and developed relationships with investment bankers and industry analysts, who could funnel them deals. I spent the majority of my time on the road talking to entrepreneurs about their dreams of starting new ventures or reading books about new technologies and futurists' predictions. My approach was to identify and invest in other people's dreams. In another organization, team members would pass by my office, catch me reading a book, magazine, or trade journal, and comment, "There he is again, doing nothing but reading. You must not have enough real work to do." I once heard a boss of mine say to a peer, "Ted works long hours, but I don't know what he does." Inspiring words from your leader! (So, another reason I'm writing this book is to inform people about what I do with my time!) In *Develop*, I'll share what I've learned over many years of soaking up all the thinking on success while advising thousands of people on how to reach their potential. The book serves a wide audience and is designed as a reference or manual you can revisit during major career transitions. You can benefit from these tools whether you're just starting out in your career or looking for your next step after working for years. In later chapters, I provide examples for those who are looking for their first job and guidance for people hunting for executive-level positions.

The book is organized into two parts. Part I outlines the seven tools. These tools are designed to broaden your perspective about development, show you how to advance your career prospects, and help you better communicate your unique gifts to others.

In chapter 1, you'll learn how to figure out what you really want and how to sharpen your own perspective using the Job Exploration Summary tool. The tool gives you a simple framework for discovering what interests you and how to articulate that interest to others in a way that engages them to help you. I continue to be amazed at the number of people who never think about what others want. Chapter 2 discusses the Constructive Questions tool, which helps you to uncover the employer's perspective and assess your fit for a job.

The next chapters cover steps you can take to advance your career prospects and communicate your unique gifts to others. Communication, you'll find, is key. I can't give clients skills and experience they don't have, yet they are more successful after working with me. In chapter 3, you'll use the Mapping Your Experience tool to describe what you

7 Tools to Take Charge of Your Career

#	Tool
1	**Job Exploration Summary** Broaden your perspective about development and career options by focusing on what you are willing to explore.
2	**Constructive Questions** Uncover the employer perspective to evaluate the fit between the role and your experience, knowledge, and skills; identify areas for development.
3	**Mapping Your Experience** Turn resume accomplishments into transferable experience and skills to communicate your talents more effectively and facilitate career transitions.
4	**Networking Quadrant** Create a blueprint for networking you will actually enjoy, and produce the results you want.
5	**Leadership Preferences Survey** Identify your leadership style and better communicate the value you bring to an organization or team.
6	**Spheres of Influence** Craft the image you want and develop the connections you need to achieve your long-term career goals.
7	**Development Plan** Create a simple but effective plan for learning both inside and outside your job and identify the one thing that would position you for a greater role.

have done without using jargon, fifteen-minute explanations, or poor examples. It helps you translate your accomplishments into transferable skills so you can connect with a wider audience. Chapter 4 shows you how to network the right way to get the help you need using the Networking Quadrant tool. Chapter 5 helps you identify what type of leader you are and what to do with that information by taking the Leadership Preferences Survey. In chapter 6, we'll talk about cultivating your image and why it becomes increasingly important the higher up you go in an organization or social system. The Spheres of Influence tool helps you assess your level of influence today and provides a road map for expanding it over time. And chapter 7 wraps up Part I by showing you how to use the Development Plan to grow in your current role.

Part II of the book discusses special considerations beyond the seven tools that are critical to consider for career development. Chapter 8 covers making transitions. Moving from one industry to another is one of the most difficult situations people face; in that chapter we'll talk about specific strategies to handle that. Finally, chapter 9 discusses the unwritten rules and obstacles faced by people of color and women as they rise through the ranks. They can't always play by the same rules as their majority and male counterparts. I try to tackle reality as it exists today, with the hope that this chapter will seem antiquated and unnecessary over time.

So, there are a couple ways you can read this book. The first is to start at the beginning of chapter 1 and read the entire book to the end. The advantage of this approach is that you will get the relationship between the seven tools. Although presented independently, the tools build on one another and mirror the process a person would take if they were identifying job opportunities, interviewing and getting a job offer, and then developing in their new role.

A second way to use this book is as a reference guide. If you are in the middle of a job search, or want help dealing with a specific situation, refer to the Quick Start Reference Guide in Appendix B. I've grouped exercises and tools around typical situations. Find the one that applies to you, and you'll find a page number for the part of the book that addresses that situation. I've created these tools in the hope that they will serve you again and again as you navigate your career.

And now I've come to the final reason I am writing this book: to serve others. I come from a family of teachers and preachers, so helping others seems to come naturally. I can honestly say that I get as much or more satisfaction seeing someone else grow and succeed as I do with my own accomplishments. I've had the privilege to advise and counsel so many people, from politicians to entrepreneurs, from artists to athletes, from executives to high school students. I'm pleased you've allowed me to be a part of your journey.

So, let's get started.

PART I

The 7 Tools

CHAPTER 1

Job Exploration Summary: Sharpen Your Own Perspective

If you don't know where you are going, you'll end up someplace else.

—*Yogi Berra*

Development is an important aspect of your career path, but you may not have a clear idea of what it is—or how you do it.

Let's get started by understanding the components of development and why each is important.

$$Development\ (x) = Experience + Time + Mastery$$

Development is a function of three interrelated components: experience, time, and mastery. You need all three to have meaningful and lasting development. It starts with experience.

I define experience as any endeavor where you see the full arc of setting an intention, doing a behavior, and observing its impact. Whether we call it a strategy, goal, purpose, plan, or reason, we want *something* to happen or occur. Then we choose a set of actions, behaviors, or approaches to achieve our goal. Finally, we see the results, consequences, outcomes, or effectiveness of our behavior.

Often, we will label an experience as "positive" if our behavior leads to the desired impact and "negative" if our intention is not met. Viewing experience through this lens is often a mistake.

When I owned a consulting company, I participated in a peer-to-peer group in which business owners got together to discuss ways to grow revenue and improve our sales techniques. One exercise that had a great impact on my outlook was the Feeling Journal. At the end of every day, I rated that day on a scale of one to ten, with one being a terrible day and ten a great day. Next to the rating I wrote a short sentence explaining why I felt that way. Typical entries for me would be: "two—did not get the Massachusetts Bay Transit Authority (MBTA) sale today, just talked about products." Or "eight—got a signed contract to run a seminar in Connecticut." Then, "ten—sold a six-month engagement to the MBTA."

After sixty days of keeping this journal, the facilitator for our group asked us to share and review our journal entries. He said, "Ted, I see you rated that day in May a ten because you signed a long-term contract with your client, the MBTA. But I also see that two months earlier, you rated your day a two because you met with the leadership team at the MBTA but did not get a sale. So, would you have gotten your sale in May without that meeting two months earlier?"

Of course, the answer to that question was no, that meeting laid the foundation for getting the sale. So, the facilitator said, "I guess that day two months ago was not really a two, and May was a ten because of that day. The point is you don't know how one experience leads you to success, so always think of every day as a ten."

That is how I want everyone to think of experience, the largest component of development. Every experience in your life has led you to this point, this moment of reading or listening to these words.

Let's put it another way. Imagine you are taking your first golf lesson. After the club pro shows you how to stand, hold a driver, and swing, you walk up to the ball, hit it, and it goes one hundred yards. You continue the lesson, and by the end of sixty minutes you are hitting the ball two hundred yards fairly consistently. Do you go home and tell friends you are a golfer? Probably not. This example may sound silly, but in the work environment, employees will often say they know how to do something after having one or two experiences. When I interview candidates, I will say, "I see on your resume you are an expert in project management [or fill in the blank], so how many projects have you led?" And the response I get back is that they've led one or two projects. Development requires a number of diverse experiences to make strong connections between our behavior and results. If we do something once and have a positive result, we may think we know why it worked, but we don't. Statisticians call this "correlation but not causation." Diversity of experience is important. To understand why, let's go back to the golf lesson. Can you hit the ball two hundred yards with different clubs? When it is windy? How about the final day of a tournament when spectators are watching? It usually takes a number of experiences, in situations with varying conditions, to have effective development. In this book I will share how to mine your experiences to see patterns of success and how to communicate those patterns to others so you can control your future career opportunities.

The second component of development is time. Intuitively we get that it takes time to develop even if we don't understand why. Imagine that two kids who have never run in their life spend an equal amount of time preparing for a 5K road race. The first child runs for two hours a day before the race. The second child, starting six days before the race, runs for twenty minutes a day. Who do you think will perform better on race day? Most people, and research, will say the second child. Time matters. In development, time allows for reflection, context, and awareness so that you can uncover insights—to discover what actions worked and why. Time helps transform the experience into development. It also takes time to see how your actions fit into a broader narrative and place events into perspective or context. In the golf example, most students would prefer to have ten one-hour lessons to prepare for a tournament than one ten-hour lesson. Time helps the learner understand the degree to which individual factors played a bigger role in performance—the weather, club selection, arc of swing, mental or physical fatigue.

Armed with this information, the golfer now has situational awareness and can focus their behavior on the next lesson or practice to achieve better results. Time is needed to evolve our personal mindset to recognize and react to various situations. Coupled with experience, time helps us get into the right mindset to use the most effective approach to a task.

The third component of development is mastery. Mastery is the ability to perform consistently at a high level over an extended period of time. It is the evidence that your development efforts have been successful. In a variety of situations, under different levels of intensity and settings, over a number of years, you can deliver positive results.

While it is nice to have an overview of why experience, time, and mastery lead to development, it is conceptual. This understanding does not directly give you the job, role, or situation you want or need to develop. To accomplish that, we need to use the exercises and tools—the first of which is the Job Exploration Summary.

In my thirty-plus years in business, I would say the single biggest obstacle to having a rewarding career is not knowing what you want, or being unable to effectively communicate what you want. A small percentage of people have always known what they have wanted to do when they grow up. Often, they are doctors, lawyers, athletes (the hard-working ones with real talent), and performing artists. But if you're like most of us, you have no clue. Maybe you started out wanting to be a fireman or nurse, graduated to superhero like Batman or Wonder Woman, and then finally focused on whatever vision your parents, teachers, or mentors saw in you.

I say this because it is okay not to know what you want (on the inside), but few people can help you unless you give them a clue. They are not mind readers, will get frustrated trying to guide you through your thought process, and will quickly lose interest. When working with clients, I want to know the answers to two critical questions:

1. What motivates you and makes you happy?
2. What are you interested in and willing to explore?

These are softer questions that don't connote a lifelong commitment. It helps people understand that there is an emotional and a functional side to any job. Achieving high levels of job satisfaction means addressing both questions, but I start with their motivations.

What Motivates You and Makes You Happy?

Frederick Herzberg, one of the most influential management thinkers, used the term "two-factor theory of job satisfaction."[1] Based upon his research, Herzberg did not see job satisfaction as one big, continuous spectrum. Instead, satisfaction and dissatisfaction are separate, independent measures. It is possible to love and hate your job at the same time. According to Herzberg, the two types of factors that determine our satisfaction and dissatisfaction are "hygiene" and motivators. While Herzberg used the term "hygiene" to mean core to your job health, I will use the term "must-have" job factors.

Must-have factors are parts of your job that, if not done right, will cause you to be dissatisfied. Examples of must-have factors:

- **Compensation**—a minimum level of pay you need to live, no matter how much you love the job and daily work.
- **Job Security**—the stability of the industry in which you work and the job you have; everyone has their own "set point" for security.
- **Work Conditions**—the surroundings of your job; some people like and need to work outdoors, others in an office, while others prefer to work at home.
- **Status**—the prestige related to the job, your title, and day-to-day responsibilities; some people require a certain level of status attached to their work to feel valued.
- **Work Location**—where you work and the length of your commute.

Motivators, on the other hand, are the things that will truly, deeply satisfy you if they are parts of your job. Examples of motivators, according to Herzberg:[2]

- **Challenging Work**—work that is exciting and develops new skills; work that tests a person's mental, physical, and/or emotional abilities.
- **Recognition**—work that is part of a larger mission or goal; work that makes a direct impact on the financial health of an organization, or being recognized and rewarded for a job well done.
- **Responsibility**—the opportunity to be in charge of people, resources, and projects; the satisfaction of delivering results and being seen as a leader.
- **Personal Growth**—work that helps you develop as a person; the job allows you the opportunity to use your strengths daily and provides insight into your weaknesses and ways to address them.
- **Mentor/Sponsor**—people value a mentor who will help them improve their knowledge and skills, or a sponsor who looks out

for their career and proactively advocates for promotions and special projects.

Discovering Your Factors

The first exercise I give clients is to review the list of choices and identify their top five must-have factors. They represent things that the job must offer for you to be happy. They should be the nonnegotiable aspects of the role. If the job does not have these aspects, then it is a signal to you to start looking for a different opportunity.

With that as guidance, review the list of choices in figure 1.1 and identify your top five must-have factors. Then write down those top five factors using the Must-Have and Motivating Factors worksheet that follows. It is not necessary to rank your must-have factors in any particular order. The goal is to create an overall picture of the mandatory parts of your job.

Next, I ask people to review the same list and identify their top five motivating factors. Motivating factors are things that would truly and deeply satisfy you. A particular role may not include all of your top five, so I do encourage people to rank their motivating factors in order of preference. With that as guidance, review the list in figure 1.1 and identify your top five motivating factors. Then write down those top five factors using the Must-Have and Motivating Factors worksheet.

Figure 1.1 is not an exhaustive list of work motivators but is a good guide for making your initial choices. Often people start with this list, reflect for a few days, and then change or add other motivators. If you don't see what motivates you on this list, just add your own motivator. It is important to define your motivator, not just put down a word or phrase. The definition will help you communicate your ideal work environment to others.

After clients complete the exercise, I paraphrase the list into a short story that describes the client's work environment. I request that they listen to my words, and at the end I ask, "Does this sound like you?" If it does, then we are good; if not, then we have more work to do to get the environment right.

Figure 1.1.

Work Motivators*

- ☐ **Autonomy:** the chance to work on projects alone
- ☐ **Challenge:** doing work that is not routine
- ☐ **Clearly defined responsibilities:** expectations are not ambiguous
- ☐ **Creativity:** the possibility to implement my own ideas
- ☐ **Decision-making authority:** the ability to make decisions
- ☐ **Diversity of tasks:** the involvement in a variety of projects
- ☐ **Expert coworkers:** to be surrounded by intelligent coworkers
- ☐ **Fame/notoriety:** to be recognized as an authority by coworkers
- ☐ **Flexibility of schedule:** the ability to shape my own schedule
- ☐ **Fringe benefits:** medical and dental insurance, paid vacation time, etc.
- ☐ **Geographic location:** choosing where I work and where I live
- ☐ **Good supervision:** direction that is accessible, clear, supportive, etc.
- ☐ **Intellectual stimulation:** work that mentally challenges me
- ☐ **Interdisciplinary:** work with exposure to different professions and areas
- ☐ **Job security:** stability in my employment and position
- ☐ **Lack of stress:** an atmosphere without a lot of deadlines
- ☐ **Leadership:** the opportunity to take charge of projects
- ☐ **Power:** the ability to create change
- ☐ **Professional expertise:** the ability to become an authority
- ☐ **Respect:** admiration by coworkers and superiors
- ☐ **Salary:** a wage consistent with my work quality
- ☐ **Seeing things through:** the ability to work on tasks from start to finish
- ☐ **Social justice/change:** making a difference by my work
- ☐ **Support:** understanding and reinforcement for my goals from coworkers
- ☐ **Teamwork:** being part of a group that works together

*Adapted from Marianne Able Career Services Center,
Thomas Jefferson University

Worksheet 1: Must-Have and Motivating Factors

Must-Have Factors (that must be right for you to be happy)

1. _____

2. _____

3. _____

4. _____

5. _____

Motivating Factors (things that truly, deeply satisfy you)

1. _____

2. _____

3. _____

4. _____

5. _____

Cindy was a graduate school classmate of mine. She is a fun, smart person who loves dance, particularly the ballet, and has a sharp eye for detail. When Cindy and I spoke about looking for another opportunity, she was working as a management consultant at a large consulting firm. Although good at the work, she was not happy in the job and was searching for a change. Check out figure 1.2, Cindy's factors chart.

Figure 1.2. Cindy's Factors Chart

Cindy's Must-Have Factors (if not done right, she'll be dissatisfied)	Cindy's Motivating Factors (things that will truly, deeply satisfy her)
1. **Respect:** admiration by coworkers and superiors 2. **Support:** understanding and reinforcement for my goals from coworkers 3. **Decision-making authority:** the ability to make decisions 4. **Geographic location:** choosing where I work and where I live 5. **Fringe benefits:** medical and dental insurance, paid vacation time, etc.	1. **Intellectual stimulation:** work that mentally challenges me 2. **Seeing things through:** the ability to work on tasks from start to finish 3. **Challenge:** doing work that is not routine 4. **Salary:** a wage consistent with my work quality 5. **Job security:** stability in my employment and position

To summarize, Cindy is looking for coworkers who admire and support her work. She wants the ability to make decisions, control where she works, and be given excellent fringe benefits. To be truly happy, Cindy wants challenging work that she can see through to the end. Finally, she wants job security and to be compensated fairly for her work. Do you see the problems I did . . . ?

Think about the life of a management consultant and Cindy's must-have factors: Respect—check, consultants are highly respected in the business world for their intellect and ability to solve problems. Support and fringe benefits—check, consultants are generally compensated well and work well in teams. Decision-making authority—now, that is a problem in consulting. You make recommendations and share insights as a consultant, but rarely do you get to make decisions. Control of where you work and live—not if you're a consultant. You can often live where you want, but the job requires extensive travel; it is not unusual to leave Sunday afternoon and return home on Thursday night. This forces consultants to live in major airline hub cities like Chicago or Atlanta. The consulting job only satisfies three (or 60 percent) of Cindy's must-have factors.

Now let's examine the motivating factors. Consulting work is generally intellectually stimulating and challenging. Often, you have to go into an unfamiliar situation, quickly assess what is wrong in an organization, and make recommendations to address the issues. The salary is also good in large consulting houses with ample opportunities for bonuses. Seeing things through, however, is a problem. Consultants work on engagements but rarely get to implement their recommendations or find out if their suggestions lead to the results predicted. This is a problem for Cindy. Job security is also a problem. Consultants always worry about their position. It is an "up or out" culture where you progress to the next level or are expected to leave the firm. Job security is tied to selling existing clients more services and finding new clients. Economic downturns disproportionally affect the consulting industry as large companies cut back spending on external vendors in such times. Like the must-have factors, consulting satisfies 60 percent of the things that would make Cindy deeply satisfied.

Completing this one exercise allowed Cindy to give voice to why consulting was not a good choice for her. She could do the job, but that is not the same as wanting to do a job.

I meet many clients who feel stuck in a role, but they can't say why. Taking the time to understand your motivations is a good first step. Before you send off tons of resumes, answer online postings, or interview for a job, can you articulate in a few sentences what you need from a job (must-have factors) and what aspects of a job would make you truly satisfied (motivating factors)?

Cindy found a new job on her own; I just helped her to identify her motivators and job aspirations. She is now the Director of Category Management, Sourcing, and Procurement for Great Dane, a manufacturer of trailers for the transportation industry. I think her new role will be a better fit than her previous consulting roles, increasing the probability of higher job satisfaction and success.

Once you complete this exercise, you can use these factors to assess whether your existing role is a fit. You can also compare one job with another and project your level of satisfaction if you accept a new position. When you start a new job, revisit your factors and rate how well the reality of the new job meets the factors at the three-, six-, and twelve-month marks. Cindy can use this exercise to evaluate her job annually to ensure it is meeting her expectations. You can use this exercise to get yourself on the right track and to monitor that your role continues to satisfy you as time passes.

It is important to revisit your factors over time because they can change. I once worked with someone on an organizational redesign project for a managed-care company. We were part of a new project team and just getting to know each other. I asked one person how he came to the organization. He said that before this job, he was a management consultant who traveled around the country. He loved the job because it was creative, challenging work that paid well. He was having breakfast with his wife and son on a Saturday morning when his son asked his wife, "Will daddy be at my game tomorrow?" His wife replied, "Yes."

He turned to his wife and said, "I can't be there tomorrow; I'm traveling to a client."

"Oh, he doesn't mean you," his wife replied. "He means our neighbor who also has a son on the team." That day, his must-have and motivating factors changed, and he left that job within six months!

Clients ask me if they should only take a job if it meets all of their must-have factors. I tell them it is okay to take that job as long as they understand it will not lead to long-term satisfaction. Think back to summer jobs you had in high school or college. We often have positive memories of those because we knew they were ending. In a few months we were going back to school. When you have a job that's low on must-haves, it is important to focus on learning as much as you can, as quickly as you can, while you create an exit plan. I've seen people get stuck in jobs because they become comfortable with a certain salary, or they accept that the job does not meet their needs. In human resources, we call these people "retired in place (RIP)."

With a good understanding of your must-have and motivating factors, you are ready for my first tool: completing your Job Exploration Summary.

The Job Exploration Summary

After counseling thousands of people and seeing the blank stares and looks of desperation on their faces when asked what job they want, I've stopped asking that question. Clients find it difficult to answer the question because they think too narrowly about career paths. To help my clients, I get them to equate development and job exploration with the creative process. Creativity requires divergent or expansive thinking before converging on a particular path. In development, that means expanding your possibilities.

During the school year I'm often asked to speak to junior high and high school students about careers. Most of these talks involve a professional sharing their story of how they got the job they have today, going through a PowerPoint presentation that describes their job responsibilities, and/or giving a commercial for the organization. As you can imagine, I don't see enthusiastic faces of young students eager to start careers in healthcare or retail. I do something different. I start by asking what careers they are interested in. Invariably, I get the usual responses: professional football or basketball player, doctor, musician, engineer, lawyer, and so on. When I ask about which companies they want to work for, the response rate goes down significantly.

These meetings are held in conference rooms or education classrooms. To make my point about expansive thinking and get the energy up in the room, I hand out a sheet of paper that has lines numbered one to thirty. I ask the students to pick a partner, and they have five minutes to walk around the room and nearby area and write down the names of thirty companies they see. The first team to complete their sheet gets a prize. At first, the teams look confused and unsure of what to do. "Someone made that chair you're sitting on," I start shouting. "How about that TV monitor? What's the name on that wall?"

Within ninety seconds, students are running around the room, turning over chairs, getting on their knees looking under the table, and going outside the room and into the hallway.

When the students come back and compare results, they are amazed at the number of different companies. This is a list I made from just one room:

1. Aetna, a CVS Health Company—health insurance
2. Andover Controls—energy solutions
3. ASP.NET—server controls
4. Avaya—voice and data communications
5. Coca-Cola—beverage
6. Crestron—building controls
7. Dove—chocolate owned by Mars
8. DVIT—differential video imaging technique
9. Green Guard—organization promoting health
10. Gyration—computer input devices
11. Hartford Builders—contractor
12. HBF—furniture/textiles
13. IBM—technology and consulting
14. JVC—television and screen technology
15. LG—electronics
16. Lenovo—computers
17. Limitimer—local area network and wide area network solutions
18. PepsiCo—snack and beverage
19. Planters—division of Kraft Heinz
20. Polycom—video, voice communication
21. Purell—hand sanitizer
22. Quaker Oats—food owned by PepsiCo
23. Revolabs—audio-visual equipment suppliers
24. Rubbermaid—household goods
25. Samsung—electronics
26. Siemens—engineering company
27. Sony—electronics
28. Steelcase—furniture company
29. Sub-Zero—kitchen appliances
30. Underwriters Lab—safety consulting and certification

I ask the students if they recognize the company names. Many have never heard of the organizations on their list. Today, most students have smartphones, so I ask them to find the websites of unfamiliar companies and read about what they do.

This simple exercise expands their universe of possible jobs and businesses. The insight increases the probability of landing the job that is right for you by getting exposure to many different types of industries, companies, and roles.

The Job Exploration Summary is a tool to help you answer the question: "What are you interested in exploring?" In my work I've found it easier for job seekers to compare one job with another to discover their true interests. The process of comparing jobs allows people to better understand which elements of a job they like and which don't appeal to them. The Job Exploration Summary is shown in worksheet 2. It has two parts: your perspective and the employer's perspective. First, we will focus on the left-hand side of the tool: how to identify and describe your perspective. Then we will discuss the employer's perspective.

Like binoculars or a zoom lens on a camera, I like clients to start at a high level and zoom in on what interests them. To do that, I get them to focus on the big picture first, then zoom in to their specific job interests. So for now, we're only looking at "Your Perspective" in this tool. The first part of the summary sheet is the industry section. I ask clients to identify three industries that they are interested in exploring.

If the person is currently in a job, I ask them to list the industry it represents. For example, if someone is a nurse, he or she might write down "healthcare." If they work for a bank, they might write "financial services" or "banking." Next, I ask: "What other industries interest you?" About half the clients I work with find this easy to do; the other half struggle. They tell me they don't know or have never thought about it this way, or just list the industries they have worked in previously. It is important to identify what you are attracted to at this point. Direct experience in the industry is not necessary. Our goal is to unlock potential areas of passion and interest. We will get practical in the next two sections. If you are stuck, a final suggestion is to look at *Fortune* magazine's list of the five hundred largest organizations. This annual report is a good way to review a listing of industries and get profiles and information on the largest organizations within that industry.

Worksheet 2: Job Exploration

Your Perspective	Employer Perspective

Your Perspective

Identify three industries/areas you are interested in:

1.
2.
3.

Identify three companies/functions for each industry/area:

1.
2.
3.
4.
5.
6.
7.
8.
9.

Identify three roles/jobs you are interested in:

1.
2.
3.

Employer Perspective

Identify top five experiences for your roles:

1.
2.
3.
4.
5.

Identify top five types of knowledge/skills for your roles:

1.
2.
3.
4.
5.

List the education you need for your roles:

1.
2.

The next section of the Job Exploration Summary is the company section. For each of the industries you identified in the first section, list three companies you admire in that industry. To help the job seeker complete this section I ask the question: "If you remained in your current industry, but did not work for your company, who would you want to work for?" Clients often have trouble identifying companies because they are using the filter of where they believe they can work. A typical response is: "I was going to say Disney, but I can't move to Florida—my kids are in high school." I interrupt them and repeat that the goal is to select organizations that they admire, whether or not it makes sense to work there. The goal is not the practical exercise of identifying potential employers but instead to crystallize the type of work environment that appeals to you.

I find people have difficulty articulating the culture, employee brand, and leadership style they are attracted to; but they find it easier to say they admire Amazon or Starbucks, for instance. The companies serve as a proxy or image of the ideal situation. The company image connects the wants of the job seeker with the network of the person trying to assist them. In our healthcare example, the nurse might identify the Cleveland Clinic, Kaiser Permanente, and the Centers for Disease Control as organizations he admires. Our financial services person might list American Express, Bank of America, and PayPal as organizations she respects.

The final part of understanding your perspective is the roles section. To complete this portion, ask: "What three jobs or roles would I like to do?" Like the company section, the goal is not only to list jobs you are qualified for today, but to uncover the type of role you would enjoy. The roles you identify signal what you would like to do daily. They highlight the scope of your responsibility and how your job fits into the overall strategy of the organization. I often find this to be the easiest section for clients to complete. In our healthcare example, the nurse could list nurse case manager, marketing, and quality assurance as three roles of interest. The financial services person might list loan officer, operations manager, or wealth advisor as potential roles.

But what if you like your company and don't want to leave? This is also common. If this describes your situation, you can modify the exercise by identifying the areas that interest you instead of industries. In healthcare, for example, are you more interested in the front office (sales, marketing, underwriting), middle office (clinical, network, or pharmacy), or back office (claims, member services, or enrollment)? If you were a banker, you might select commercial, retail, or investment banking.

If you don't want to change companies, identify the functions or sub-areas for each of the areas. If you were interested in sales, for instance, you might be interested in individual, small group, or large account sales, or account management. If commercial banking sounded appealing, you might identify credit analysis, account management, or loan origination as possible areas of interest.

The roles section is likely to be the same as someone exploring other industries, but if you know you want to work with your current company, you can go deeper. As a current employee you probably have access to the internal job-posting site. If so, review open jobs and identify the specific ones that interest you. Often companies have a place where you can download job descriptions, whether or not there is an opening. These descriptions provide valuable information.

It is important to understand which of the three components are most important to you—industry, company, or role. In my work with clients, I find they have a natural tendency to prioritize one component over the others. Some people want to work in a particular industry—say entertainment. They are less concerned about which company they work for or what role they have. Others want to work for a specific company—say Google—for its culture and brand. They are open to multiple roles if it is with their target company. Others prioritize the role—say marketing manager—and they are willing to change companies or industries to keep the role.

You've now completed the left side of the Job Exploration Summary tool by articulating your perspective of what you want. See figure 1.3 for an example of a completed left side of a Job Exploration Summary.

You've completed your perspective, but this is only raw data. We must turn that information into a format that allows others to help us find the right opportunity. If you filled out all of the sections on the left side of the Job Exploration Summary tool, you have identified twenty-seven different jobs. You unlock those jobs by combining the three sections into one sentence. I ask people to create three Job Aspiration statements to explore. The format is:

I am interested in exploring . . . [role] in the . . . [industry] with a company like . . . [company]."

In the case of our nurse, he might say: "I am interested in exploring a nurse case manager role in the healthcare industry for an organization like the Cleveland Clinic." Our banker might say: "I am interested in exploring an operations manager role in the financial services industry for a company like American Express." These simple, direct sentences help others quickly identify contacts by painting a vivid picture of what they are looking for. Images of friends and contacts they know pop in their head. Based on their statement, people often will say, "I know a nurse case manager," or "I know someone at American Express," or "I have a friend in the healthcare industry."

Figure 1.3. Sample Job Exploration Summary

Your Perspective	Employer Perspective
Identify three industries/areas you are interested in:	**Identify top five experiences for your roles:**
1. Financial Services	1.
2. Healthcare	2.
3. Entertainment	3.
	4.
Identify three companies/functions for each industry/area:	5.
1. American Express	**Identify top five types of knowledge/ skills for your roles:**
2. Bank of America	1.
3. PayPal	2.
4. Cleveland Clinic	3.
5. Kaiser Permanente	4.
6. Centers for Disease Control	5.
7. Disney	
8. Comcast	**List the education you need for your roles:**
9. Amazon	1.
Identify three roles/jobs you are interested in:	2.
1. Wealth Advisor	
2. Chief Financial Officer	
3. Operations Manager	

Other sample Job Aspiration statements:

- I am interested in exploring a wealth advisor role in the financial services industry with a company like Bank of America.
- I am interested in exploring a chief financial officer role in the entertainment industry with a company like Disney.

- I am interested in exploring an operations manager role in the healthcare industry for an organization like the Centers for Disease Control.

These statements are a good place to start when networking, a topic I cover in chapter 4, and during informational interviewing. They start the conversation and can be used to get information for how to develop in your current role and prepare for your next role.

But what if you know what kind of job you want? You aren't just exploring, but actively job hunting. In this case, I ask clients to modify the job statements into aspiration statements for their next job.

The goal is to describe your next job aspiration. It expands on the simple exploration statement by including what makes you qualified for the job. It should include a) time frame; b) role/job scope; c) situation; and d) what differentiates you (unique strength and experience—more on this shortly).

Example:

Within three years, become the Business Unit CFO for a Fortune 100 health services company that utilizes my corporate development strengths and seven-plus years of accounting and debt-structuring experience.

This simple one-sentence statement contains all the elements of a good aspiration—time frame (within three years), role (Business Unit CFO), situation (Fortune 100 health services company), unique strength (corporate development), and experience (seven-plus years of accounting and debt structuring experience).

Clients I work with often resist writing these statements. They don't want to limit their options, or say they are open to different types of jobs. I reassure them that this specificity helps them in the long run. First, you don't have to limit yourself to a single statement. I have clients write one statement for each of the roles they identified on the Job Exploration Summary in worksheet 2. Then I share a story that illustrates my point.

I was having lunch with three associates in our Finance Leadership Development Program. The program accelerates the development of high-potential talent to take on leadership roles within the function. They wanted my advice on career development. What courses should they take? What business unit was the best place to work? Did they need to manage people in their next role? I said, "It depends. What is your career and job aspiration?" Without hesitating, all three said they wanted to be chief financial officers (CFOs). They pressed for answers to their questions. I said I needed more information, shared the format of the aspiration statement, and gave them a few minutes to write an answer. One asked, "What do you mean by unique strength?" To answer that question, think about something you do or know better than 85 percent of the population. That is a unique strength. The percentage is not really important, it just gives people a perspective of what I mean by unique. They continued writing.

As our lunch arrived, I asked each to share their sentence. One wanted to be the CFO of a large Fortune 500 company. Another wanted to be the CFO of a midsized company. The third person wanted to be the CFO of a venture capital firm. I smiled and asked them to eat their lunch and I would share my thoughts.

"Fifteen minutes ago," I said, "all of you thought you were in competition with each other because you wanted the same role—CFO. Now you see that each of you has a different situation, which has a profound impact on your development. The person who wants to be the CFO of a Fortune 500 company will need to gain experience in corporate finance roles like internal audit, budgeting, and investor relations in addition to working as a business unit CFO for our large commercial business. The person who wants a midsized company is better off working for our specialty businesses where they control more operational levers and function like a small independent company. Stints in places like investor relations would not be necessary if working for a private company. Finally, the person interested in the venture capital firm will need experience in our corporate strategy and development areas to give him exposure to mergers and acquisitions. The clearer your aspiration, the easier it is to tailor your development to achieve your goals."

So, you are ready to interview for a new role, right? Not quite! You have incomplete information and it is only through your lens. You are ready to network and research, not interview. One of the biggest mistakes I see clients make is ignoring the employer perspective. This important viewpoint is the subject of the next chapter. To complete the right side of the Job Exploration Summary, we need to know how to ask the right questions to uncover the information you need. The Constructive Questions tool uncovers those answers.

■ ■ ■

Use the left side of the Job Exploration Summary tool to create job aspirations that summarize what you are willing to explore. Intention is blind unless well communicated. Share your aspiration with people who work in your desired industry, work at your desired companies, or have your target job.

Bottom line: Expand your options, don't limit your thinking.

CHAPTER 2

Constructive Questions: Design Your Bridge

Most of the successful people I've known are the ones who do more listening than talking.

—*Bernard M. Baruch*

Workers often ignore or can't articulate what employers want and managers expect. This results in development and job-search guesswork. Solely basing your understanding of an employer on Google searches or asking a hiring manager questions at an interview is a big mistake. Many candidates believe using social media gives them an edge. After looking through my LinkedIn profile, videos on YouTube, and Google searches, a potential candidate feels confident they have the information necessary to bond with me and build rapport. They are rarely correct, and the information they have gathered makes them come across as stiff (or, worse, like a stalker). A couple of examples will illustrate this point and what not to do in an interview.

I had a candidate who reviewed videos and speeches of my CEO prior to our meeting. During our conversation, she pulled out a legal pad with numerous questions. Glancing at her writing, I said, "It looks like you have a number of questions about the job. Please share and I will try to address them."

"Given the recent passage of the Affordable Care Act," she began, "what are your thoughts on how that will affect Aetna's product offerings?" Next, she asked, "What is our acquisition strategy?" Finally, she offered ideas for improving our operations.

Given these questions, you might think I was interviewing her for an executive-level position, right? No, it was for an eight-month administrative contract-worker assignment.

There is nothing wrong with doing homework on your interviewer or target company. The purpose of your research is not to look smart or strategic for its own sake. Research should provide insight into your role and responsibilities. Your questions help you understand the scope of the role, what success looks like, and the support you can expect.

I have an iPod in my office that often plays background music—classical or jazz most of the time. I find it relaxes those who come to see me. One client asked where the music was coming from. When I pointed out the iPod, she asked if she could see the device. Surprised, I handed it to the young lady, who proceeded to review its contents. She said you can learn a lot about a person from their music and began to ask me questions about my taste in rap, country, and classical music. I was happy to answer her questions, but I am certain it did not help her identify her next job.

Not all information is good information or appropriate for a job or networking interview. Social media is a great tool for uncovering personal connections between people, understanding interests, and gathering general information on a company and its strategy. But at the end of the day, clients are interested in a certain role, in a particular industry, with a specific company. Interviewing and networking needs to focus on these three components. I call this "getting the employer perspective."

At the end of chapter 1, you created three job statements to explore. Now it is time to get the employer perspective of what they are looking for from an ideal candidate. Once you know this, you can design and build a bridge from your skills and experience to the new role. You also can address any gaps that may exist. That is why I refer to the Constructive Questions tool as designing your bridge; chapter 3 will describe how to build the bridge.

Put Yourself in the Employer's Shoes

To get started, it is helpful to put yourself into the employer's shoes. To do this, imagine you own a restaurant and you are hiring a chef.

The first thing you want to know from a candidate is, "Do you have experience as a chef?" The answer to that question is a simple yes or no. If yes, then you will ask follow-up questions to probe that experience. Has the candidate run a kitchen for the type of restaurant you own, or is this a new situation? Is their experience with a larger, smaller, or same-size restaurant? Was the old restaurant a success? Why or why not? You get the picture. You have many different areas to discuss, but your questions stem from the fact that they answered yes to the question of having direct experience as a chef.

If the answer is no, then you want to know: "Do you have the knowledge and skills to be successful as a chef?" The answer to this question is also a simple yes or no. If yes, does the candidate have knowledge about cooking, menu creation, and/or managing people? Have they developed cooking skills by catering on the side, working under another chef, or throwing elaborate parties in their home? You want to know if the candidate has the knowledge and skills so if you give them the job, there is a high probability of success. Their skills are a good predictor of success in the absence of direct experience. This occurs often when we apply for a new job or push for a promotion. We don't have direct experience, but we try to signal to others that our knowledge and skills should give the hiring manager comfort. You are hiring based on "potential" versus demonstrated past performance.

If the answer is no to experience and no to knowledge/skills, then you want to know: "Do you have the education needed to develop the necessary knowledge and skills?" You would ask if the candidate was a food science major in college, or if they've graduated from culinary school. This situation often applies to those who are early in their career. They are often frustrated because employers want experience, but they can't get experience unless someone hires them. It is a Catch-22 that we all must go through. If you hired a candidate to be your chef who had no experience, only education, it would be because you liked them and wanted to take the risk. The decision you made was personal and probably based on a feeling or circumstance. Because it was intuitive, it is often isolated and not repeatable. That is what is frustrating about being young and/or inexperienced. We all need a lucky break to get started in an industry or at a company. How others got a job or break will have little resemblance to how you will get started. In the long run, the laws of probability work in your favor. The more employers you connect with and the more roles you apply for, the more likely you are to succeed. See figure 2.1 for a summary of the employer interviewing flowchart.

Figure 2.1. Employer Interviewing Flowchart

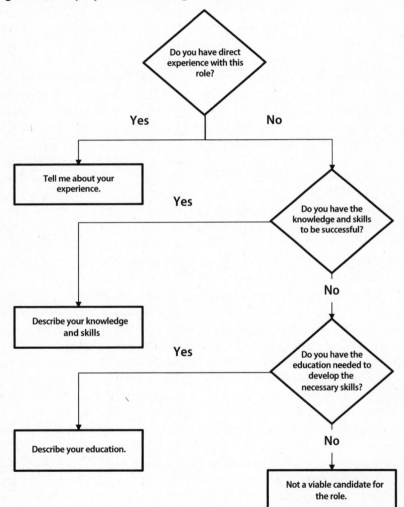

To continue our restaurant manager example, imagine you have hired your new chef. Depending on your personality and circumstance, you took a chance on someone, hired based on their knowledge and skills, or hired someone with a proven track record.

Now we can connect the concepts of the employer perspective with your job statements.

Constructive Questions

Before you interview for a job, it is time to reach out to workers who hold the role you've described to get the employer perspective. When I counsel clients, they often fill out the employer side of the Job Exploration Summary sheet. I ask them where they got the information for the employer side, and 99 percent of the time they say, "I filled it in myself."

How would you know what to write if you've never had the job? A lot of people will say they read the job description. The trouble with job descriptions is they are often out of date, written by human resources and not someone who has actually done the job, and the qualifications outlined describe the perfect candidate. You have to talk to and network with people in the field. I will explain in more detail about networking in chapter 4, but let's assume you have identified someone with the job you want. They have graciously agreed to meet you for coffee for thirty minutes. What is the best use of that time? Reviewing your resume?

To start, I encourage clients to gather information, do as little talking as possible, and build a bridge between your aspirations and what the employer is seeking. I ask clients to use the Constructive Questions tool (figure 2.2) to get the most out of their conversations.

Figure 2.2. Constructive Questions

Experience Questions:

1. What are the top five types of experience an ideal candidate would have for this role?

2. Looking back, what experience prepared you the most for your current role?

3. If you had ten years to train someone for an executive-level job in your area, what assignments would you give them, why, and for how long in each role?

Knowledge/Skills Questions:

4. What are the top three skills an ideal candidate would have for this role?
5. Looking back, what knowledge prepared you the most for your current role?
6. What two skills, if mastered, would set me apart from others in this industry?

Education Questions:

7. What are the minimum education and certification requirements for this role?
8. How does a person with this education approach problems and opportunities differently than people from other disciplines?

Since experience is the most important component, you should start your conversation around this topic. These are the questions I suggest and why they are important.

1. **What are the top five types of experience an ideal candidate would have for this role?**
   This question helps identify what type of experience is valued most by the organization. Imagine you are interested in a marketing role with Coca-Cola. The ideal candidate might have extensive marketing-strategy experience—creating a market-entry strategy for a new product. Or campaign-management experience—launching a new advertising campaign for a mature product. Perhaps market-research experience is most valued in the role—gaining insights from focus groups and sales data.

The Trait/How	Bridge to Get to What	What
Strategic	What kind of strategy?	Marketing strategy for a new product.
Leadership	What will this leader need to do in the first six months?	Build a new go-to-market team.
Collaborative	Who will we work with and why?	Work with sales team to increase revenue.
Detail-Oriented	Quality sounds important; who sees this person's work?	Prepare documents for CEO and senior leaders.

It is important to probe for "*what* the ideal candidate does" and not just "*how*," or "*a trait* the ideal candidate uses to do it." This point is very important. Use the chart on the previous page to better understand the difference.

2. **Looking back, what experience prepared you the most for your current role?**
   If you are interested in the role of the person you are speaking with, this question requires them to reflect on their career progression. It is rare that we can accurately gauge the importance of an assignment in the moment. In hindsight, however, we can pinpoint the people, situations, and assignments that helped us grow. We see which skills and knowledge bases are used most often.

3. **If you had ten years to train someone for an executive-level job in your area, what assignments would you give them, why, and for how long in each role?**
   This question focuses on development and the future. It forces people to think about a natural career progression. Many employees feel stuck in a role because they don't see a logical career path to where they want to go. This question allows you to get one person's perspective on a successful career path. Asking multiple employees to answer this question allows you to construct a potential career path at the beginning of a job.

   It also corrects a common mistake I see candidates make by asking, "Tell me about your career path." People love to share their experiences and reminisce about the good old days. You will get a lot of information, but it might not help your development. What you want to know is what will work in today's environment, not what worked in the past.

   Finally, this question gives you a sense of what is most important by asking about the amount of time spent in each role.

Gaining the required job experience for your target opportunity does not require the same investment in time and intensity across all roles. Some experience you can gain by participating on a project team, while another requires years of dedication and practice. When working with a client, I get them to distinguish between three levels of experience:

- **Level 1 Experience**: At this level, what is most important is that you gain enough experience so you understand the role and its significance, and have the ability to hire good people. To be a chief financial officer of a Fortune 500 company, you may have worked on a special project with internal audit, but you don't need to have a full-time job in internal audit. As a CFO, you will hire specialists in this area.
- **Level 2 Experience**: At this level, it is important that you have direct experience in this role and the ability to differentiate among great, good, and poor performance. Using our CFO example, I want you to have experience in the major areas that drive company performance. That might include stints in investor relations, financial planning and performance, and risk management.
- **Level 3 Experience**: This is your towering strength. To give clients a sense of what I mean, I ask them: "What do you know how to do better than 85 percent of people?" You have a track record of success. In our CFO example, the towering strength could be the ability to turn around a mature business. The person would be able to give at least three examples of reinvigorating a stagnant business.

Next you want to probe deeper on the knowledge and skills needed to be successful in this role. This is the most important focus area if you are transitioning from one industry to another or from one function to another. You are listening closely so you can build a bridge between your skills and the new area. You can't draw upon direct experience, so you must rely on skills and knowledge. The next questions will reveal important insights.

4. **What are the top three skills an ideal candidate would have for this role?**
   This question helps you home in on what is important. Job descriptions can be intimidating with their laundry list of skills the candidate should possess. If you have 60 percent of the overall skills listed, it is worth a discussion. But it is important to have 95 percent

of the most important skills. Get people to list the top three skills so you can map them to your background. Imagine you are interested in transitioning from a freelance writer to a corporate communications role. The most important skills might be a) written and oral communication expertise; b) editing communications on short notice; and c) the ability to build relationships and collaborate with other communications professionals.

Armed with this information, when it comes time to write your cover letter or go to the interview, you can provide examples of freelance work done on short notice that required collaboration with others. You can also share diverse samples of your work to highlight your written skills. The discussion will serve as a test of your oral communication skills. Your goal is to control the interview by focusing on the most important skills, which you have, and not the laundry list of nice-to-have skills that are mentioned in the job description.

5. **Looking back, what knowledge prepared you the most for your current role?**
If you are interested in the role of the person you are speaking with, this question uncovers the knowledge—as opposed to the skills—that helped them achieve success. In our corporate communications example, knowledge of social media tracking software could be an answer. Knowledge of public affairs or community relations would be other examples.

Knowledge is equivalent to level one or two experience. You know enough to tell great from good from poor. Collecting this information will help you denominate the value of gaining extra knowledge. You can prioritize conferences you attend, books you read, and people you network with based on assessing how the knowledge is valued.

6. **What two skills, if mastered, would set me apart from others in this industry?**
This question focuses on development and the future. What worked yesterday will not necessarily work in the future. The goal is to focus your development on skills that matter. Gathering a diverse set of viewpoints will allow you to discover which skills matter most.

The final area of the employer perspective is the education needed for the role. Suggested questions, with their importance:

7. **What are the minimum education and certification requirements for this role?**
   Most jobs have a required level of education. In the corporate communications example, a college degree is required. Some jobs will use the word "preferred" instead of "required" to signal that certain experiences are viewed as more important. People often ask me if they should go back to school and pursue a certain degree or level of education. Get the minimum level of education required for the highest level of job you wish to apply for.

   In my case, I have a master's in business administration because this degree will allow me to rise to the level of CEO in most Fortune 500 organizations. Not having an MBA would exclude me from consideration for key roles. On the other hand, a doctorate is nice to have but not necessary. I had the opportunity to stay and earn my doctorate but determined that I didn't need it to achieve my goals (and spared my wife and myself from more debt). On the other hand, if I had stayed in the education field, a doctorate would have been necessary to give me access to university-level positions or the highest administrative-level positions in public schools.

8. **How does a person from one educational background (e.g., engineering) approach problems and opportunities differently than people from another background (e.g., economics)?**
   This is important information to have so you understand how employees think and act. Consider the scenario where you graduate from college at age twenty-two, and you work until age sixty-two. You spent forty years working but only four years in college and three years in your major field of study. But during those forty years, employers kept asking you where you went to school and what you majored in. Schools and major field of study influenced the roles employers thought you could fill. So, there must be something more important about education than meets the eye.

   The answer is how the discipline approaches opportunities and problems. I was an economics major in college. Economists, in simple terms, review data, look for historical patterns, and then create mathematical models based on those patterns to predict future events and trends. Behavioral economists look to find predictors of human preference and decision-making. So, if you hire an economist, you expect them to approach problems and opportunities analytically, make data-driven decisions, and build strategies based on statistical models.

This question gets employers to share the mindset the ideal candidate brings to the role. Once you know that mindset, you can describe how you have used that approach in the past to deliver results. You don't have to be an economist to share examples of when you made data-driven decisions or built statistical models.

Using the Constructive Questions tool and getting answers to the eight questions highlighted in this chapter will give you a clear picture of what an employer is looking for in a given role. Remember that you don't have to have the same person answer all of the questions; you want to speak to a few people to get diverse viewpoints on what you need.

The best time to set up informational interviews and use the Constructive Questions tool is *before* you apply for open jobs or when you are exploring a career change. A simple analogy would be giving a music recital or performance. Informational interviews are like dress rehearsals. You are in a real environment (talking to someone who is a hiring manager), but you are practicing and getting feedback that you will use during an actual job interview.

Applying for an open job and asking employers what they are looking for during an interview is like performing without a dress rehearsal. Your questions will confuse the interviewer. The *job interview* is the time to show that you are the best candidate for the role. The *informational interview* is the time to find out what experiences, knowledge, skills, and education the best candidate should possess. It is important to separate the two interviews.

Armed with data from informational interviews, you can now realistically compare your experience with the employer's perspective. With your informational interviews completed, we can circle back and finish the Job Exploration Summary we started in chapter 1. Figure 2.3 shows a completed summary using the example of a person wishing to become the CFO for an entertainment company. Based on interviews, they have learned the most important experiences, knowledge, skills, and education needed to get that role. Remember that the goal is to then compare your actual skills with the desired skills. If there is a 60 percent or greater match, it is worth it to pursue the opportunity.

Figure 2.3. Revisiting the Sample Job Exploration Summary

Your Perspective	Employer Perspective
Identify three industries/areas you are interested in:	I am interested in exploring a chief financial officer role, in the entertainment industry, with a company like Disney.
1. Financial Services	
2. Healthcare	
3. Entertainment	
	Identify top five experiences for your role:
Identify three companies/functions for each industry/area:	1. Negotiated foreign distribution deals
1. American Express	2. Financial leader at Fortune 500 company
2. Bank of America	3. Worked with board of directors
3. PayPal	4. 10+ years entertainment experience
4. Cleveland Clinic	5. CFO for start-up venture
5. Kaiser Permanente	
6. Centers for Disease Control	**Identify top five types of knowledge/skills for your roles:**
7. Disney	1. Production financial modeling
8. Comcast	2. Film and television finance
9. Amazon	3. Merger integration skills
	4. Negotiating tax incentives
Identify three roles/jobs you are interested in:	5. Risk management
1. Wealth Advisor	**List the education you need for your roles:**
2. Chief Financial Officer	1. Bachelor's degree—finance, accounting
3. Operations Manager	2. MBA or JD preferred

Using the Constructive Questions tool helps you uncover what employers are looking for and allows you to fill out the right side of the Job Exploration Summary tool.

■ ■ ■

Stella came to Aetna as part of an international acquisition. She worked as a medical officer for the company we acquired. Prior to Aetna she worked for the Arabian Health Service in Dubai, UAE. At Aetna, Stella held clinical operations and care-management roles. When she came to me she was looking for a change. While she liked her current role and teammates, she felt stuck.

We started with her aspirations. Stella was looking for a new role—one where she had the power to create change and make a difference. Also, a role that was intellectually stimulating and required creativity. But she did not know where to start. Next, we used the Job Exploration Summary tool to expand Stella's options. She initially focused on international jobs, but after a couple of sessions, Stella was willing to consider nonprofit health organizations and corporate social-responsibility roles. Stella was one of the people who had filled out the right side of the Exploration Summary tool based on her understanding. When I asked, "Where did you get the information to fill out the employer perspective?" she replied, "I filled it out."

I told her she could not speak from the employer perspective. I encouraged her to network with hiring managers to see what they needed. Stella was a diligent networker who would check in with me to debrief her conversations. She talked to people both inside and outside of the international division. After a few months, Stella got a job offer to be the Senior Director of Clinical Health Services. It was a lateral move but offered an increase in pay and the opportunity to work in one of the fastest-growing areas of our domestic operations. It also fulfilled her motivating factors, as she will help develop, influence, and implement medical cost strategies and initiatives to improve population health.

Stella sent me an email when she accepted the role. "Thank you very much for all your guidance . . . It was your push which propelled me to start exploratory meetings and I was fortunate to come across this opportunity very early in the exploratory phase."

Bottom line: Don't guess—get perspective from people doing the hiring.

CHAPTER 3

Mapping Your Experience: Build Your Bridge

We build too many walls and not enough bridges.

—*Isaac Newton*

At this point in your journey you are almost ready for that job interview. You can articulate your desired work environment because you've identified your must-have and motivating factors. You've thought broadly about the industries, companies, and roles that interest you and narrowed down your options by creating job aspiration statements. You've conducted informational interviews with workers in your target field who have shared the experiences, knowledge, and skills and education you'll need to be successful in the role. Preparing for the actual job interview is the next step. The Mapping Your Experience tool will get you ready. It gives you the language to communicate the talents you will bring to the role and the value you will bring to the organization.

Before I share the tool, I want to talk about the proper mindset and approach to interviews and resumes. Understanding what resumes and interviews are and are not will help you be better prepared.

Successful interviews are a result of good preparation and the ability to distill a lifetime of experiences into digestible ninety-second to three-minute stories. Ramble on too long and people will forget the main points of your answer and their attention will lapse. If your answers are too short, you risk coming across as stiff and not likable.

The STAR Method

To prepare for an interview, create three ninety-second stories that address the major experience themes you uncovered in your fact-finding discussions. I tell people to use the "STAR Method" to ensure they have a full but concise response:

- **Situation**: Outline the situation—when, where, etc.
- **Task**: Review the specific tasks you were given and what your supervisor or client expected you to do.
- **Action**: Share the major actions you took to accomplish the task.
- **Results**: Describe the results or impact of your work.

The STAR Method will prepare you for the majority of interview question types. I tell clients that any answer must cover all four components of the method. The interviewer's question will tell you where to start. An example will make this point clearer. Imagine you are applying for a sales job at OfficeMax, a large office supply company. Your current job is in sales with a smaller competitor, W.B. Mason, and now you would like to work at the larger organization. One of your resume accomplishments is as follows:

"I was working as a store manager in Rhode Island when I was asked to join a project to increase sales in the New England region. I was responsible for leading the five-person team that developed a new sales, distribution, and promotion strategy in ninety days. We implemented the new strategy last year, and overall sales have increased fifteen percent year to date compared to the same time period last year."

This one concise story addresses all of the following types of prompts:

- *Describe a situation when you were asked to do something above and beyond your day-to-day responsibilities* (situation). In this case, start with the situation and cover all the other points: "I was working as a store manager in Rhode Island when . . ."
- *Tell me about a time when you worked on a team project, what went well and what did not* (task). In this case, start with the task: "I was responsible for leading a five-person team charged with increasing sales in the New England region . . ."

- *Do you have the ability to work under pressure without perfect information* (action)? In this case start with the action: "I had to develop a new sales, distribution, and promotion strategy in ninety days; the situation was . . ."
- *Tell me about one of your greatest accomplishments* (result). In this case, start with the result: "I increased sales by fifteen percent year over year; the situation was . . ."

Interviews are about communicating the important components of your experience, then providing details based on the interviewer's follow-up questions. The most common mistakes I see made by candidates are talking too long, providing too many details, and not directly answering the question asked.

Candidates usually talk too long because they are trying to describe all their experience in one meeting. RELAX and just STOP! There is no easy way to share a lifetime of experiences, successes, and knowledge in thirty or sixty minutes. You are far more accomplished than that. Shift your mindset. Your goal is to provide highlights or a snapshot only. You do this by sharing ninety-second to three-minute stories using the STAR Method. Then listen, really listen to the interviewer to see what they are interested in. You can tell because they will use phrases like, "Tell me more about . . ." or "How did you do that . . ." That is your cue to provide more details and begin a two-way dialogue. Using the STAR Method, followed by supporting information, you will come across more relaxed, natural, and accomplished.

Candidates often provide too many details because they are nervous. They want to impress others by providing all the context and information on their resume. It also fills the silence, which makes people feel better. The problem with this strategy is that you are guessing what is important to the interviewer. If you guess wrong, you are rambling on about something that is not of interest, and the interviewer will be tuning you out or wondering when you are going to stop talking. It sounds scary, but it is much easier to have a dialogue by listening, responding, and being open to where the conversation takes you.

Another common mistake is not directly answering questions. You are not a politician on the campaign trail reframing interviewers' questions so you can give your stump speech. Listen to the questions and answer directly. If the question is confusing, ask for clarification before answering. It is a mistake to use the phrase: "I'm not exactly sure if this is your question, but I think. . ." Encourage the interviewer to use different words or give you a hint of what they are looking to understand about your experience. Then you can answer appropriately. In the case where you don't have an answer to a question or you don't know the answer, say: "Good question, I'll have to get back to you." Then get back to the interviewer as quickly as possible. I am always impressed by a candidate who provides supporting information and perspective after an interview. It signals their professionalism and follow-through.

Basic Resume Principles

You're walking into the office of a hiring manager. She or he rises to greet you warmly and shake your hand. You see a copy of your resume on their desk and you sit down. Now what?

First, we need to share some truths about resumes—what they do and don't do. Except for very technical jobs and unusual situations, you will never get a job or promotion based on a resume. In most cases, a resume will not land you a job, but it can eliminate you from consideration. I am not going to give detailed guidance on writing resumes. A simple Google search on how to write a resume returns more than 400 million hits! What follows are the most important principles I've found helpful to clients:

1. **Make sure your resume does not contain spelging— I mean spelling—or factual errors.**

   The resume is a screening device for talent acquisition recruiters. They are not looking for reasons to hire you but ways to eliminate you from contention. Errors and misspellings are an easy way to weed you out. Since a resume alone will not get you a job, there is no reason to stretch the truth on a resume. Factual errors and exaggerations will come back to haunt you.

   Keep it as short as possible. The goal is not to tell your life story, just to get employers interested in talking to you. For each job, your resume should highlight accomplishments, not provide a blow-by-blow description of how you did your job. It should include your company, role, a one- or two-sentence description of your job responsibilities, and a list of accomplishments. If you have worked less than five years, try to keep your resume to one page, two pages for up to fifteen years, and three pages for sixteen-plus years.

2. **Prepare for a behavioral assessment.**
Most interviews are based on the principle that the best predictor of future behavior is past behavior. Therefore, recruiters will ask you about prior work experience and focus on your behaviors, or how you completed your work assignments. They assume if given a new task you will act in a similar way.

3. **Assume the person you are speaking with has not read the resume.**
Hiring managers and professionals are busy. A conscientious person will read your resume, but the majority of interviewers will skim the resume five minutes before you walk into their office. A signal that this is the case is the common first question: "Tell me about yourself." In response, provide a nice, concise two-minute review of your work history and education.

4. **Scope, budget, and people are important if you are seeking a manager-level job.**
When applying for management positions, don't make the interviewer guess. The resume should clearly outline the scope of your job responsibilities, the size of the budget you managed, how many employees directly reported to you, and how many employees were in your span of control. There is a big difference between managing a $5 million budget with three employees who report to you directly and managing a $15 million budget with seven direct reports.

5. **Executive-level jobs require a "wow" factor.**
If you are seeking an executive-level job, the resume should highlight the biggest accomplishment in your roles and its organizational impact. The impact should focus on a) increased revenue or

profit; b) increased quality; c) reduced costs; d) improved level of service; or e) increased efficiency or effectiveness.

6. **Update your resume every year.**
It is painful to watch clients who have not updated their resume in years try to remember what their accomplishments were. Update the document while your accomplishments are fresh in your mind. It is often difficult to get the budget and people numbers accurate after a couple of years. Many financial and HR systems update in real time, eliminating historical snapshots of information.

Mapping Your Experience

When interviewing, there are two basic situations you will encounter. The first is when you have direct experience with the role you are apply-ing for. The other is when you don't have direct experience, but you have related experience, knowledge, and skills. The Mapping Your Experi-ence tool is helpful in both situations, but it's more important if you don't have direct experience.

The salesperson applying for the OfficeMax job is an example of someone who has direct experience. In this scenario, your job during the interview is to listen carefully to discover what is most important to the interviewer. You already have the experience and you've highlighted your accomplishments, so you need to address the interviewer's stated and unstated questions. If you are unsure, ask—don't guess. A couple of examples will make this clear. If the interviewer says: "I see you were able to grow sales in New England, but that is a small market for us," then you might say: "It sounds like you want to know how I would pro-duce the same results in a larger market, is that correct?" If the inter-viewer agrees, then you can answer the question directly and share why you are ready to work in a larger market.

On the other hand, if the interviewer says: "A marketing plan in ninety days would be impossible in our organization," the person could be asking about cultural fit. You might say: "Each organization is differ-ent, and it sounds like more people would be involved in the decision-making process at OfficeMax, is that correct?" With that understanding you can assure the interviewer that you are adaptable to different work environments, cultures, and decision-making processes.

The key insight I want you to have is: **If you have direct experience, then you already possess *what* they are looking for, so focus on cultural fit, your working style, boss relationships, and other aspects of the job that focus on *how* you get results**.

Now let's tackle the scenario where you don't have direct experience. This situation requires a little more work on your part and greater influencing skills. The key insight is: **If you don't have direct experience, you must identify and communicate transferable experiences, knowledge, and skills**.

This scenario is frustrating to clients who often ask: "How can I get experience if they don't give me a job first?" Before introducing the Mapping Your Experience tool for addressing this problem, it is good to understand why people think so narrowly when hiring in the first place.

If I hire someone who has direct experience and went to the right schools, the assumption is that person will have a higher probability of success. Most people understand and believe this logic. If the person succeeds in the role, then it validates the hypothesis. If the person does not perform well, then the failure is attributed to the individual. The hiring manager says, "I don't know what happened. They had the right experience and background." If on the other hand you take a chance on someone with an unusual background and they don't succeed, then the failure is attributed to the hiring manager. People say: "Why did you hire that person? They did not work out."

The hiring manager is taking a greater risk in this scenario. In this case, hiring a person who does not have direct experience is analogous to adopting a new innovation. You are the innovation. When I use the term "innovation," I like Everett M. Rogers's definition, which is an idea, practice, or object that is perceived as new to an individual or group. I like this interpretation because it broadens a person's perspective of what qualifies as an innovation and focuses that perspective from the customer's point of view. An innovation does not have to be groundbreaking or novel using this definition. If something is new to a group, it may qualify. In the case of the manager hiring a person with experience from another industry, that outsider qualifies as someone new or innovative. Like an innovation that hasn't been introduced yet, you are "invisible" to the hiring manager because you don't have the exact industry experience. Until they can "see" you, human resource recruiters and interviewers will pass by you. As a job seeker you can't get frustrated; it is a natural human reaction. You just need tools to get employers to see you as a solution to their problem.

To illustrate this point, I share the example of the evolution of the use of air-conditioning. Willis H. Carrier applied for a patent for his air-conditioning system in 1904. The system was originally designed to solve a problem in the printing industry. Humid weather degraded the quality of color printing. Carrier, an engineer working for the Buffalo Forge Company, was asked to devise a system that would dehumidify and clean the interior air of a printing company in Brooklyn, New York. After 1904, the following uses for air conditioning were introduced:[3]

1919:   The first air-conditioned movie theater opens in Chicago, Illinois.

1919:   The first air-conditioned department store, Abraham & Straus, opens in New York City.

1929:   The first fully air-conditioned high-rise structure opens in San Antonio, Texas.

1931:   The Baltimore and Ohio Railroad introduces air-conditioning to the railway industry.

1939:   Packard introduces air-conditioning to the automotive industry.

1940:   Greyhound introduces air-conditioning to the bus industry.

Each introduction of air-conditioning was an innovation that transformed a particular industry and its customers. Note that it took twenty-seven years to put air-conditioning in a railroad car. It took an additional eight years for the innovation to migrate from a railroad car to a passenger car. Notice, however, that it took only one year for air-conditioning to migrate from a car to a bus. To introduce air-conditioning to the railroad business, management had to explore innovation occurring outside of their industry. Someone had to ask, "If they can put air-conditioning in a building, couldn't we put it in a train car (in essence, a moving building)?" Since most managers look only to competitors and industry leaders for innovation, the value of air-conditioning was probably not widely understood in the railway industry prior to Baltimore and Ohio's introduction. It would transform not only what could be transported on rail, but how far.

The migration of air-conditioning from car to bus occurred in only one year. In this case, the industries are complementary, and managers of these companies are more likely to monitor each other. Organizations that successfully manage the innovation process consistently look both within and outside their industry for innovations. Something that is old hat and commonplace in one industry can be a breakthrough in another setting or environment.

To successfully get employers to hire you when you have different experience, you need to build that bridge from your skills to the needs of the new role. In human resources, we call these "transferable" skills and experience.

To identify transferable experience and skills, we will use the Mapping Your Experience tool (see worksheet 3).

Worksheet 3: Mapping Your Experience

Resume Accomplishment

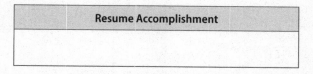

Transferable Skills to Achieve Accomplishment		Key Milestones to Reach Accomplishment	
1.		1.	
2.		2.	
3.		3.	
4.		4.	
5.		5.	

This tool helps you analyze your resume accomplishments, then turn them into transferable experiences and skills. Get out your resume and write one of your accomplishments in the top box. For illustration, I will continue the sales example: our W.B. Mason salesperson wants a job as a project manager for an auto parts manufacturer. Using the tool, we populate the accomplishment and then list the top five skills used to achieve that goal (see figure 3.1).

Figure 3.1. Mapping Your Experience: Example

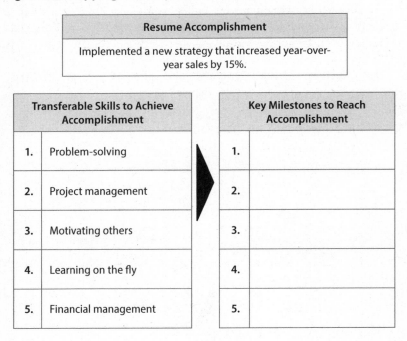

Resume Accomplishment
Implemented a new strategy that increased year-over-year sales by 15%.

Transferable Skills to Achieve Accomplishment		Key Milestones to Reach Accomplishment	
1.	Problem-solving	1.	
2.	Project management	2.	
3.	Motivating others	3.	
4.	Learning on the fly	4.	
5.	Financial management	5.	

Next, we list the top five milestones to accomplish the goal. Think of milestones as concrete work products or outputs that people would recognize as steps to realizing the goal. Figure 3.2 shows the complete mapping.

Now the salesperson can go into the interview and build a bridge from their current sales job to the new project manager job. In an interview, our salesperson can say: "A successful salesperson, like a project manager, needs to learn on the fly, be a good problem solver, and know how to motivate others. I used these skills to grow our New England sales by fifteen percent and am confident I can help your organization achieve its goals."

Our salesperson needs to persuade the interviewer to have a more holistic view of their experience. In the interviewer's mind, direct experience means a candidate has done the exact same job in the exact same industry. The milestones represent transferable experience. The salesperson can build that bridge by saying things like: "I believe good project managers have experience defining a problem, analyzing that problem, developing solutions, getting buy-in and funding for the solution, and implementing and measuring results. Do I have that right, or am I missing something?" When the interviewer agrees, the salesperson can continue saying: "I have direct experience guiding a project

Figure 3.2. Mapping Your Experience

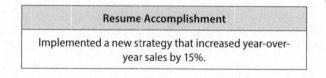

Resume Accomplishment
Implemented a new strategy that increased year-over-year sales by 15%.

Transferable Skills to Achieve Accomplishment		Key Milestones to Reach Accomplishment	
1.	Problem-solving	1.	Conduct market analysis
2.	Project management	2.	Create sales projections
3.	Motivating others	3.	Develop distribution strategy
4.	Learning on the fly	4.	Get corporate funding
5.	Financial management	5.	Launch promotional campaign

through all those phases. Let me tell you about a time when I led a project team to increase revenue by fifteen percent . . ."

If you are not actively looking for a new job, then use the Mapping Your Experience tool in a slightly modified way. Imagine our W.B. Mason salesperson, but in this scenario, he is not looking to leave the organization. You would fill out the tool the same way, but the discussion changes. You set up a development conversation with your boss or mentor. You review your accomplishments, transferable skills, and key milestones. Your goal is to get feedback. Ask the following questions:

1. *From your perspective, are there other accomplishments that you believe to be more significant or impressive?* Use this question to validate your accomplishment.
2. *What behavior/skills did you observe?* Get input on what others see. Often others see and appreciate other skills that we miss or take for granted.
3. *Where can I use my skills to solve a current problem or take advantage of an opportunity?* The answer to this question will give you ideas for how you can add new value in your current role and set you up for future success.

■ ■ ■

Your goal is to make your experience relevant and accessible to the interviewer. The Mapping Your Experience tool takes the jargon out of your resume accomplishments so more employers understand how your past success is relevant to current opportunities and problems.

When I work with leaders with a strong technical background, I focus on the Mapping Tool. Those who work in information technology, finance, and legal professionals are a few examples. Soldiers transitioning from the military into civilian roles also fit in this category. It is important to translate your experience into accomplishments and responsibilities others can understand. Tell employers *what* you know how to do, the *resources* you control, and the *results* you deliver. A couple of examples will help you get started:.

Old Language:	Squadron Section Commander for the Air Force
New Language:	I manage twelve operational initiatives (*what*), six direct reports, and a $20 million budget (*resources*), to prepare our unit for combat (*result*).
Old Language:	Information Technology QA Release Manager
New Language:	I make sure the software and operational systems for our new line of sneakers (*what*) support the sales team's projections (*result*) with my four-person team and $5 million budget (*resources*).

Bottom line: Focus on what you know how to do using simple language.

With a better, more nuanced understanding of the employer perspective and how to prepare for interviews, we can expand the opportunities available to us.

In these last two chapters, we've been talking about building a bridge between your experience and an available job. Part of that involved interviewing the people doing the hiring—in other words, an entrée into networking. Networking is the best way to find more and better opportunities, whether in your current organization or outside your company. Networking with the right people is critical to your success and the subject of the next chapter.

CHAPTER 4

The Networking Quadrant: Forge Strong Connections

Networking is rubbish; have friends instead.
> —*Steve Winwood, British musician*

Tina, a finance leader, sat in my office and said, "I know I need to reach out to people; I just am so busy." Two months had passed between our first development conversation and this one. She wasn't happy with her current job but did not know what to do.

Another client, Celia, was the head of operations, compliance, marketing, and client service for an asset-management firm when she came into my office. This business unit that managed hedge fund portfolios was going to be closed, her job eliminated. After thirteen years with the organization, she was looking for a new role and needed help. She was ready for a complete career change veering away from hedge funds. She thought she could translate her skills from serving as a chief operating officer to a foundation or not-for-profit organization but wasn't sure.

Both Tina and Celia needed more information. For Tina, it was a general question of what was next. Knowing you are not happy in your current role is not the same as knowing where you want to go next. In Celia's case, she needed information on COO jobs in the foundation space. What did they pay? Would they find her corporate finance experience an advantage? What is the best way to break into the field? In both cases I recommended structured networking to get answers to these questions and to identify and explore possible opportunities. Networking was the answer.

Everyone knows networking is good for you. You've read the articles and seen the statistics. Numerous studies estimate that between 70 percent and 80 percent of all jobs are filled via networking. But networking is like exercise: we know it is good for us, but many people stop when life gets busy, or they make excuses and don't get around to it. So, why do we have such difficulty devoting time to networking?

I believe most people hate networking because they do it the wrong way. They don't know whom to talk to, what to talk about, and how to leverage those conversations to get results. They need more structure to make the process work for them and better guidance on what to do.

At the end of the day, there are four conditions that you must satisfy for employers to do business with you: they must know you and like you, and they have to know your work and like your work. And by "do business," I mean hire you or work with you in any capacity. As with many things in life, the power and significance of this statement gets lost by its simple and direct nature. I expanded on this concept, after working with hundreds of people on developing their careers, to create a networking framework. I call it the Networking Quadrant tool (see figure 4.1), a concept I created with my colleague Bill Varnell.

The Networking Quadrants Tool

The horizontal axis of the Networking Quadrants, the people scale, represents the degree to which people both know you and like you. The vertical axis, the work scale, represents the degree to which people know your work and like your work. These two factors together produce the four networking quadrants—peer, client, traditional, and social.

In the lower left quadrant, employers don't know you well and they don't know your work. I call this the Traditional Networking quadrant because it reminds me of typical networking—and why my clients hate it! Picture yourself by your phone trying to build up the nerve to call someone you don't know. She may be an industry expert, have a job opening, or be a friend of a friend. How do you feel? If you're like most of us: nervous and anxious. Secretly you hope the person does not answer the phone as you make the call. Over the years I've read many articles that focus on giving you the courage to talk to strangers, improving your pitch, and boosting your self-esteem to deal with the rejection that comes with traditional networking. Like most of my clients, I try to avoid talking to strangers as much as possible. Isn't that what our parents told us when we were four years old?

Traditional Networking is time-consuming and not effective in the short run. There is value in getting to know new people, but it's better if you have some connection. I'll talk more about this quadrant later, but the key message is that if you are going to go through the hard work of establishing a new relationship with someone, they'd better have the potential to make a significant impact on your career.

Figure 4.1. The Networking Quadrants

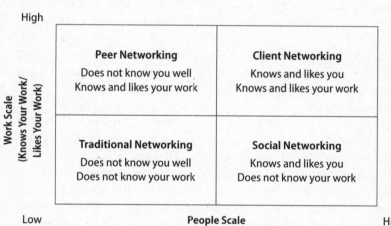

In the lower right quadrant, people know and like you but don't know your work. I call this the Social Networking quadrant because people that tend to know and like you are often tied to your social or family life. You have some natural affiliation, like going to the same school or being a part of a sports team or club. Because you see these people on a regular basis, they know you well and like you as a person. Given the social nature of your interaction, however, they don't know your work. They might have a vague understanding of your job, but you probably haven't spent the time to discuss your work in depth.

In my work with clients, I find they neglect this quadrant the most. They do that because of a faulty assumption. Clients will say to me: "But my mother/aunt/classmate doesn't know anything about my job/industry." The faulty assumption is you are looking for a direct connection between what you are seeking and the person. What is important is not *what* they know but *who* they know. You are tapping into their network.

In the upper left quadrant, people know and like your work but don't know you very well. I call this the Peer Networking quadrant because the people that often fit this description are your work peers. It's easy to picture colleagues you have worked closely with for several years— spending long hours, sometimes nights or weekends, getting a project completed. These colleagues know and trust your work and value your contributions to the team. They can effortlessly explain your expertise to others and give examples of your accomplishments. But they are often the inverse of your social quadrant friends. They have a vague knowledge of your personal life, your spouse, kids, hobbies, and history unless you purposely cultivate this area.

In my work I've found that clients overvalue their Peer Network and undervalue their Social Network. Peers are important, but you must take specific steps to ensure you get the full value from work colleagues and others whom you've worked with closely.

People in the final quadrant in the upper right know and like you and know and like your work. I call this the Client Networking quadrant because they represent the people who have partnered with you to achieve your best results. They enjoy working with you. Your success has also helped them succeed. You care about them both as individuals and as work partners. Together you have faced and overcome challenging times and benefited from good times.

I use the word "client" instead of "customer" purposely. The *Merriam-Webster* dictionary defines a customer as "one that purchases a commodity or service." It implies a transaction. A client is defined as "one that is under the protection of another . . . a person who engages the professional advice or services of another." When it comes to networking, you want to connect with people who see you as an advisor who has their best interest at heart, not just someone who has used your products or services. This difference in meaning will become important as you look for another role or the opportunity to grow in your existing role.

Introducing the concept of quadrants leads to more strategic and nuanced networking. Instead of creating a random or disconnected list of contacts you want to speak with, the quadrants help you organize your network based on how they can assist you. You increase the efficiency and effectiveness of networking by identifying contacts who already know you or your work well. People in three of the quadrants already satisfy at least two of the four conditions mentioned, so you can focus your conversations. In traditional networking, you are trying to get people to know you, have a positive impression of you, understand what you are looking for, and know your work all in one thirty- or sixty-minute conversation. This is a difficult task that most clients shy away from. Using the networking quadrant, we recognize that each section has different needs. You can change your strategy and activities based on that understanding.

Each Quadrant Has a Different Target Audience

The first step is to recognize that each quadrant has a different target audience (see figure 4.2). The Networking Quadrants tool was originally created from a business owner's point of view, so I will speak both from the perspective of a business owner and from the point of view of an employee in a company.

Traditional Networking for a business owner includes sales prospects, potential suppliers, and industry experts. It involves cold calling for business, diversifying your suppliers, and making connections with people that can help propel your business. The business owner wants to target connections who can grow their revenue and profits, decrease their costs, and improve the quality of the products and services they offer. For employees, the Traditional Networking quadrant includes connections you meet at mixers and conferences and people you admire at other companies. It also includes managers in other parts of your organization. Because these people don't know you, it takes time to establish a relationship. Employees want to target contacts who can hire them or provide insight into a different industry, a specific company, or a role they wish to explore.

Social Networking is the same for business owners and employees. Contacts include family members, friends, and people you know from social settings. The people in this group know you first and foremost as a person outside of your work world. They developed an impression of you as a person first, then an understanding of your career or work. They are part of the broader community that supports you. Your goal is to target friends with large, influential networks. People in this quadrant are usually the most willing to connect you with their contacts and will speak highly of you.

Peer Networking for a business owner includes colleagues, companies that indirectly use your services, competitors within your industry, and anyone who knows your company by its reputation or brand. For employees, Peer Networking includes coworkers, people who are part of the same profession either inside or outside the organization, and anyone who has worked with you or knows your work by reputation.

Figure 4.2. The Networking Quadrants: Each quadrant has a different target audience.

	High	
Work Scale (Knows Your Work/ Likes Your Work)	**Peer Networking** • Business Peers • Coworkers • People Who Know You by Reputation	**Client Networking** • Customers/Clients • Vendors/Partners • Staff
	Traditional Networking • Sales Prospects • Industry Experts • People You Admire	**Social Networking** • Family Members • Friends • Social Contacts
Low	**People Scale** (Knows You/Likes You)	High

Client Networking for a business owner includes their best customers or clients, vendors or supplier partners, and subcontractors. For employees, Client Networking includes staff, internal departments you supply services to (if you are in a corporate function), external clients that use your products, or services and community partners. In short, all the key stakeholders that you count on to deliver value to your clients.

Now that you have a good sense of the quadrants, the next step is to understand how networking is different in each quadrant and how to maximize the time you spend networking.

Using Your Time Wisely

Your networking goal is different in each quadrant (see figure 4.3). Getting results in the Traditional Networking quadrant takes the greatest amount of time because contacts don't know you or your work. For employees, your focus should be on identifying and cultivating contacts that can have a significant impact on your career. I refer to these people as "wow" contacts. Ask yourself which people, if they were in your network, could hire you into their department? They can be a sponsor and help you get promoted. Who can help you

Figure 4.3. The Networking Quadrants: Use your time wisely.

	Peer Networking (30%) (Focus on Bonding and Rapport) • Lunches • Coffee • Social Engagements	Client Networking (50%) (Focus on Referrals and Feedback) • Customer Meetings • Referral Meetings • Feedback Meetings
	Traditional Networking (10%) (Focus on Contacts and Ideas) • Association Mixers • Conferences • Consultant Meetings	Social Networking (10%) (Focus on Connections and Trials) • Visit Your Work • Offer Free Work Sample • Introductions to Others

Work Scale (Knows Your Work/ Likes Your Work)

High / Low

People Scale (Knows You/Likes You)

Low / High

access more resources in the form of employees and/or money? They can expand your network by introducing you to experts in your field or provide opportunities for you to speak at conferences and/or seminars. In short, they can open doors for you.

If you are a business owner, your focus should be on ideas. You want to find contacts who have insight into getting new customers and opening new markets. Look for people who know proven ways to increase the size and volume of your transactions. They can point the way to adding new value that results in higher customer satisfaction, retention, and profit.

When it comes time to network, I recommend spending 10 percent of your time talking with individuals in this quadrant.

For employees, getting results in the Social Networking quadrant means focusing on connections. Since the people in this quadrant already know and like you, the focus of the discussions is on finding the connections that can propel your career. It's not who you know that is most important, but the contacts known by the people you know who are most important. You take the time to describe your work history, career aspiration, and short- and long-term goals. Then you describe the types of connections that would be most helpful. Outline the industry experience you seek, the knowledge and skills you are trying to develop, and the education you want. Next, using the experience, skills, and education lens just described, determine how the person can help you and how you can help them. The easiest way is if your social contact can directly help you achieve your goals. Another path is to review the contacts of your social network to identify those who are most promising. Ask for virtual (email, LinkedIn) or in-person connections (coffee, lunch) to get started. When you connect with those people, the goal is to bond and build rapport, not ask for a job or business. Like traditional networking, connections from your social network don't know you or your work, but you have the advantage of getting background from someone they know well. Use that information to quickly identify and leverage points of mutual interest, background, and knowledge. This will help you develop a relationship faster than the traditional networking path.

If you are a business owner, your focus should be on providing trials or samples of your products and services. You want friends in your social network to come to a deeper understanding of the value you offer clients. Start your networking by describing why you started your business. People don't buy what you do; they buy why you do it. What is the purpose, cause, or belief behind your business? Next, talk about how you do it. What sets your business apart from the competition? Finally, outline what you do. As Simon Sinek notes, great leaders inspire action by going from the inside out (why, how, what). Traditional companies go from the outside in (what, how, why).[4]

When networking, I recommend spending 10 percent of your time connecting with friends in the Social Networking quadrant.

For employees, maximizing results in the Peer Networking quadrant means focusing on bonding and building rapport. This can seem counterintuitive, but these colleagues already know and like your work. The problem is they don't know *you* well. It is important to spend the time getting to know your peers. We are social animals by nature, and we all want to be part of a larger tribe. Acceptance within the community is more about social skills. To make this point clearer to those I counsel, I share many stories about coworkers who have been laid off from work. Although hurt and shocked, they are initially confident because they have a large number of LinkedIn connections. They were hard workers with good ratings and positive reputations with colleagues. After about one or two months of searching, they share their surprise and frustration with the lack of help they have received from people they used to work with. Their former colleagues are slow to return their phone calls, offer few suggestions or contacts, and are reluctant to provide recommendations to hiring managers. The job seeker sees their network and list of contacts shrink. What happened? These colleagues know their work, have counted on them to produce results, but seem hesitant to help. The reason is they don't know you well. We don't recommend and advocate for people unless there is a personal connection—you are in a gray zone.

Ironically, it is easier to recommend a stranger than someone you are casually familiar with. In the case of the stranger, it is easy to say: "Hey, I don't know this person and have not worked with them, but attached is their resume, and on paper they look like someone you might be interested in." If I recommend someone I've worked with before, however, the first question from the hiring manager will be: "What do you think about this person?" In this scenario you are not merely passing on information. Your own reputation is on the line. This raises the stakes, so you are not likely to recommend someone unless you know both them and their work very well.

If you are a business owner, your focus is also on bonding and building rapport with the goal of deepening the relationship. Remember the difference between client and customer. Over time, you want clients to feel comfortable coming to you for advice. Their image of you evolves from supplier or vendor to a professional who protects them and has their best interest at heart. When people see you as a client, they become less price sensitive, view you as a true partner, and are more likely to become a long-term customer and to provide referrals.

Whether an employee or business owner, your job in this quadrant is to devote the time to allow people to get to know you personally. This means lunches, coffee, social engagements, etc. During these meetings, your goal is not to discuss business but to provide a window into who you are as a person. Do you have kids? What are your main hobbies and interests? Recommendations, business referrals, and recognition will all increase when people know you personally, above and beyond your work.

I recommend spending 30 percent of your networking time connecting with colleagues in the Peer Networking quadrant.

For employees, the Client Networking quadrant means focusing on referrals and feedback. These people know and like both you and your work. Encourage this group of connections to give you the honest feedback you need to develop. You will be more open to constructive and developmental feedback if it comes from people who like you. The key is to convince people in this quadrant that providing constructive feedback is more important than sparing your feelings. Clients can help to identify the strengths and abilities that you can build a career upon, as well as the behaviors that can derail your progress.

You should also share your career aspirations with people in this quadrant. If they have a good understanding of where you want to direct your career, they are more likely to take the time to refer you to contacts they know in their network and advocate for your success.

If you are a business owner, people in the Client Networking quadrant can help you grow your business in three ways. First, they are the best source of new customer referrals. Routinely you should ask: "Who do you know that has a similar problem or need that might benefit from my services?" Second, they can be a great way to understand how you can increase the size of the sales transactions. Ask them what they do before, during, and after they use your services. If you can fulfill those needs, it can open new market space. Finally, current clients can help you brainstorm new value to offer to new and existing clients and the industry.

I recommend spending 50 percent of your networking time with clients in this quadrant.

Creating Your Power Ten

One of the highest-rated programs we offer colleagues is called Executive Presentations: The Science and Art of Influence. It is designed to help participants examine the actual qualities that define executive presence and provide the tools they will need to grow and develop as leaders. During the program, participants videotape short presentations and get tips for improving their speaking techniques. The program also covers the neuroscience of influence and the transformational power of stories. I'm asked to speak to the group about networking and expanding their spheres of influence.

I start by asking who in the audience likes networking. A few hands go up, but most people are uncomfortable with traditional networking and therefore avoid or limit their time doing it. I tell them by the end of my talk they will adopt my networking quadrant approach and will find the concept of networking more manageable and less scary.

To demonstrate why the majority of participants don't like networking, I act out a familiar scene. You're at an event with a drink in one hand and a small plate of hors d'oeuvres in another. You smile, nod too much, and after a few minutes, you awkwardly fumble for and trade business cards or exchange contact information by cell phone. You get back to your office and put the business card in a drawer or fancy cardholder you got as a gift from a friend, or you email the person and say it was a pleasure meeting them. After six months, you forget the person, and after a year you can't remember why you have their contact information.

My performance always gets a laugh and not because of my acting skills. It is a familiar pattern that is played out around the world. I tell everyone there is a better way to network, and it starts by completing an exercise I call your Power Ten (see worksheet 4). Step 1 is to identify ten people you will network with over the next twelve months. Don't worry about handing out fifty business cards, connecting to one thousand people on LinkedIn, or following one hundred people on Twitter or Facebook. Instead, you should only focus on ten people at a time.

Worksheet 4: Your Networking Quadrants: Your Power Ten

High

	Peer Networking (30%) (Does not know you well, but knows and likes your work)	Client Networking (50%) (Knows you well, and knows and likes your work)
Work Scale (Knows Your Work/Likes Your Work)	• • •	• • • • •
	Traditional Networking (10%) (Does not know you or your work well)	Social Networking (10%) (Knows you well, but does not know your work)
	•	•

Low   People Scale   High
                (Knows You/Likes You)

Start off with your friends in the Client Networking quadrant. Write down five names of friends who know you and like you and know your work and like your work. The number of names corresponds to the percentage of time I recommend you spend in this quadrant. Fifty percent equates to five names, as this chart will include ten names when done. Make sure to write the names in pencil. The format should be:

Name (company, title or role)
Jane Doe (Acme, Inc., VP Marketing)

Next, in the Peer Networking quadrant, write down three names of colleagues who know and like your work, but don't know you well. This corresponds to the amount of time you will spend in this quadrant.

Two spots remain in the bottom half of the diagram. On the left side, write down the name of one person who, if they knew you and liked you, could make your career dreams come true. This is the Traditional Networking quadrant. Finally, on the right side, write down the name of a close friend or family member who knows a number of influential people. This is the Social Networking quadrant.

You now have the first draft of your networking quadrant with ten names, the companies they work for, and their roles. At this point I ask participants in the Executive Presentation course: "How did you find this exercise, was it easy or hard to fill out?" If you found it difficult, this is a sign that you would benefit from spending more time thinking about expanding your network. Identify which quadrant has the most gaps. Take the time to go through your resume and online profiles like LinkedIn to fill in any gaps.

Assessing the Strength of Your Power Ten and Making Adjustments

I had you write the names in pencil so we can make edits to strengthen your Power Ten. Consider the following questions:

1. **Do more than 50 percent of your ten names work at your current company?**

If the answer is yes, then you have too great a concentration in one company. You will not get the breadth of perspective you need to be successful when compared to others with more diverse networks. Take the time now to make changes so you have no more than five people from your current company.

2. **Do more than 50 percent of your ten names share the same work function as you?**
   If the answer is yes, then you have too narrow a focus on your area. If you are an attorney and seven of your ten names are also attorneys, your perspective will be limited. People with similar backgrounds tend to have the same level of education, knowledge of the same opportunities, and might approach challenges in the same way. Revisit your names and make changes so no more than five people come from the same function.

3. **What is your mix of men and women?**
   Does your list contain all men or all women? If so, you are missing out on another important dimension or perspective. Make edits to strengthen your list. It does not have to be fifty-fifty, just make sure you are not missing out on broader networks.

4. **What percentage of your contacts are from outside your region? Your country?**
   It's very helpful to have a diverse regional and national perspective. Depending on the industry, one region or country might be more progressive or advanced than another. Having contact with people in these areas allows you to anticipate trends and opportunities in your region. Because we have a global, interdependent economy, being part of a global network gives you an advantage. Review your list and add at least one name from outside your region and one name of someone who works in another country. If you're talking to people outside of your area often, you will have to do it virtually. To mimic the advantages of face-to-face meetings, try using video chat. If that is not available, then email a brief bio with your picture. It's important to include a current photo because it makes you "real" in the other person's mind.

5. **What percentage of your contacts are from outside your industry?**
   Just like the regional question, having contacts outside of your industry is also important. Touching base with people in other industries gives you a more holistic perspective of your role, company, and industry. It gives you information that allows you to compare and contrast the environmental trends in your field with others. If you find that your industry has the same opportunities and challenges as other industries, they can serve as a source for ideas and solutions.

Making changes to your networking quadrant based on the five questions, you now have your initial Power Ten. Let's start networking. For illustrative purposes, we will assume you are truly networking phobic and want to get the maximum impact with the minimum effort.

A Year of Networking

Go back to your Power Ten in worksheet 4. The goal is to initiate at least one interaction a month and then build off your initial ten meetings.

Start in the Client Quadrant. This should ease your anxiety because 50 percent of your networking will be in this quadrant. Set up a forty-five to sixty-minute meeting with contacts in this group, one per month during January, February, March, April, and May. As outlined before, the topic of these discussions is to get feedback and then referrals to others you should connect with. You share your career aspirations as well as the "wow" person you want to meet but don't yet know.

Next, focus on the Peer Quadrant. Set up thirty-minute meetings with each person in this group for June, July, and August. Notice that this is during the warm summer months (in the US). This is purposeful. People are generally happier and more relaxed during this time. Your goal is to have lunches, coffee, or a social gathering so people get to know you better as a person. If you are brave, hold a cookout at your home or offer to take your group out to dinner, your treat. Who is going to turn down free food from a colleague? Remember, you are not talking shop; the goal is to relax and let people see another side of you. Try to find new connections and areas of interest among your peers.

It's September and, so far, you have only talked to people you know and who know your work. Time to focus on the Social Quadrant. Set up a meeting with one friend who knows and likes you but does not know your work. This one- or two-hour meeting is a fifty-fifty conversation where you listen and find out what your friend or family member does for a living. Your goal is to listen closely to determine if anyone in your network can help. Offer assistance and contacts first. If you do, then they are more likely to open their network to you. If you own a business, offer a way for the person to experience what you do. Share a sample of your product or service. Offer a coupon to try out your restaurant or consulting service. The goal is to get people to know your work.

Well, now it's October and you have yet to talk to a stranger—don't you just love my approach! It's time for the Traditional Quadrant. It is time to review the name of the person that can transform your career or business. You've shared that name with your clients who know the person, or if not, can get you one degree closer. Schedule that twenty- to thirty-minute meeting with your "wow" contact. To make this meeting less awkward, go in prepared with a strategy. There are many, but I will share a few:

- **Warm Transfer**—If someone knows your "wow" contact, ask them to send an email or facilitate a personal introduction; either way you can spend the first few minutes talking about the person who connected you (this will ease the tension).
- **Neutral Site Meeting**—Meet at a conference, industry gathering, or business breakfast; that way the theme of the meeting can break the ice.
- **Provide Value**—Share information, perspective, or something that the person will find helpful; the goal is to show that you care to make this a win/win relationship.
- **Ask for Advice**—Who is not flattered when someone asks for their help? Present an issue or problem that you would like their insight and perspective to solve.

I am sure you can think of more examples. The key is to identify the approach that is comfortable to you.

Think in terms of 360-degree networking. People often network only with people in positions above them. Consider networking with peers and people younger or below your current position. Connections at various levels have different insights to offer.

When networking with people above you or who have more experience:

- Network with a person who recognized your abilities and encouraged you to pursue a given direction.
  The key: Ask them what they saw in you at the time.
- Network with a person who can hone your ability—an expert in your field.
  The key: Ask how they use your skills at a higher level.
- Network with a person who has a vision for your abilities.
  The key: They will expand your view of what is possible.

When networking with peers:

- Network with a person with the same abilities and passion you have.
  The key: Push each other to develop and share feedback on your progress.
- Network with a person with the same level of aspiration.
  The key: Choose a future part of your inner circle or management team.

When networking with people below you:

- Network with a person with the same talents or abilities.
  The key: Develop followers by mentoring and sponsoring the next generation of talent.

In all of these meetings, you are conducting an informational interview or actively looking for a job. If it is an informational interview, you're sharing what you are willing to explore (your perspective) and getting their input on the experience, knowledge, skills, and education needed for someone to get an expanded role or grow in their existing role (employer perspective). If you're actively looking for a job, then you want to share your aspiration statements, get the employer perspective, and/or get connected with people your contacts know that work in your target industry, work at your target companies, or have the role you are seeking.

Finally, it is important that you get the name of one person your contacts believe you should connect with in the future. Then you can update your Power Ten with a new name given during your networking. Alternatively, you can replace it with another person you know that was not in the original list of ten. Updating your Power Ten, you'll always have clear line of sight to your rolling twelve months of networking.

■ ■ ■

Let's wrap up by checking in with Tina and Celia. Celia created her Power Ten and spoke with a number of people in the foundation and not-for-profit space. She learned that it was difficult to break in, there were few opportunities, and the ones that did exist did not meet her compensation requirements. In light of this information, Celia pursued her other career aspirations and successfully landed a role as the vice president of strategy and business execution for a large healthcare organization. This job allowed her to work in a mission-driven environment that matched her values without sacrificing her compensation and benefit must-have factors.

Tina's role initially expanded to include new responsibilities, but she recently found out her job is being eliminated. She needs to take the next step and create her Power Ten. This will start her journey to find more meaningful work.

Use the Networking Quadrant to reduce the fear associated with networking. It provides structure to the different types of conversations needed for success. Remember to think of 360-degree networking to expand your perspective.

Bottom line: Success requires networking at all levels.

Networking the wrong way leads to frustration, as well as wasted time and energy. Networking the right way is efficient and effective. Use the Power Ten exercise to stay on track.

Organizations spend significant money, time, and energy identifying and developing leaders. Like the quest for the Holy Grail, they are looking for the key to attracting and retaining leaders. Well, I have a little secret about leaders, and it is the subject of the next chapter.

CHAPTER 5

Leadership Preferences Survey: Identify Your Unique Style

In my walks, every man I meet is my superior in some way, and in that I learn from him.

—*Ralph Waldo Emerson*

We are obsessed with leadership . . . we are looking for resilient leaders, accountable leaders, empathetic leaders, fierce leaders, change leaders, innovative leaders, and global leaders, just to name a few. We analyze and dissect people for leadership skills, competencies, qualities, laws, blind spots, culture, mindset, etc. There are leadership books, workshops, courses, and assessments. Kids are told they need to focus on leadership to be successful in high school. High school students must show leadership to get into the best colleges. College students need to demonstrate leadership to obtain a good job. You get the picture—leadership is important, and society wants to know how to attract more leaders and create better leaders in business, government, and not-for-profit organizations.

Because of our leadership obsession, I can't write a book about development without addressing leadership. Training and development at most Fortune 500 companies is divided between functional training, learning the technical skills needed to do your job, and leadership training to help you become a better manager and lead at a higher level. New employees want to be part of corporate leadership development programs to be on the fast track. Midlevel managers need to show they are leaders, not just managers, to get into senior management. Senior managers need to hone their leadership skills to make it to the C-suite.

Over my career, I've observed, coached, and guided thousands of people, from CEOs and presidents of Fortune 500 companies, to entrepreneurs and small business owners, to college and high school students, to government officials and politicians. I've designed, developed, and delivered leadership development programs and workshops. I've built departments and systems to identify and develop pipelines of leaders. Like others in my profession, I originally focused on identifying the most important competencies, traits, qualities, or skills of leaders. The goal was to discover leadership's secret sauce or ingredient. Once we found it, we could share that information with others and produce leaders . . . right?

Over the years my viewpoint has shifted, and I don't think this way anymore.

Today I believe leadership development is like a spiritual journey. This was my first insight. Spiritual journeys are personal and profound. Leadership, like a spiritual journey, involves complex questions, exposure to new ideas, deep reflection, and guidance from others who have been on a similar path. My aim is to share the journey and provide insights I've observed colleagues gather as they evolve to higher levels of leadership. I begin with two images to understand the nature of the leadership journey. Both are inspired by the story-meditations of the spiritual teacher and writer Anthony de Mello, in his book *Heart of the Enlightened*. De Mello was writing about spirituality, but I believe these images can apply to leadership as well.

The first image is someone climbing a spiral staircase in the dark. They don't know where the stairs lead, and as each stair is climbed, the previous step disappears.

Leadership is an uncertain journey. You don't know exactly where you are going. Often you will grope in the darkness and feel your way around. At times, uneasiness will fill your heart. The stairs can represent the corporate ladder. You will be scared when you learn there is no going back, because each step changes you. You can stop on any given step or continue to climb upward not knowing where it will lead. The most successful and influential leaders I've worked with are driven by curiosity. They are just as scared and unsure as everyone else, but their fear does not paralyze them, and they continue to explore, grow, and climb.

The second vignette is a monastery, where more than ten thousand monks are living with the Zen master Lin Chi. When the Zen master is asked how many disciples he has, he replies, "Four or five at the very most."

Many managers are attracted to the idea of higher leadership, but few put in the work to attain the goal. The message of the Zen master is instructive to me. Thousands of participants attend my leadership programs each year. Most have a positive experience and enjoy the time networking with peers and getting away from the pressures of day-to-day management. Many also appreciate the tools and tips we share and use them to achieve better results in their job. But, what I've found is similar to what the Zen master noted about the four or five true disciples among the thousands of monks: very few of the participants who attend these programs are true *disciples* of leadership.

In addition to treating leadership development like a spiritual journey, I've learned that I do a terrible job picking which participants will dedicate themselves to the journey. That leads to my second insight: my job is not to pick the leaders but to recognize the leaders—those workers who will put in the effort. The analogy I use is that those in power want to pick the winners of the horserace before the race starts. We label a select few employees as "high potential" and give them preferential access to tailored development programs and exposure to senior leaders and put them on lists as successors to leaders. The problem many companies encounter is that when they retrospectively look at who actually replaces those leaders and who is successful when promoted, they see they did not do a good job of picking the right horse. Many organizations find that jobs filled internally by those on the succession plan are in the single digits, and the success rate of promoted managers is a fifty-fifty proposition.

So, this chapter focuses on the journey you must take to become a great leader and provides you with a road map. Like a mentor on a hero's journey, I can point the way, offer words of encouragement, try to inspire you, and provide guidance when you hit stumbling blocks and barriers. But in the end, you must walk your own path and you will be proud to say, "I did it myself."

The evolution of a leader revolves around three interconnected components—mindset, the belief/behavior link, and success formula (see figure 5.1). My work with leaders centers around inspiring them to think more deeply about, and gain more experience with, each component. It is important to note that I don't generally share this model with program participants or clients but use it as a guide to understand where they are in their journey and expose them to the next step in the tower, to go back to my original analogy.

Figure 5.1. Evolution of a Leader

Mindset

Mindset refers to how leaders think about themselves. What is their attitude? Do they have a positive or negative self-image? Do they like or dislike their role in the organization? What is their attitude in relationship to their company and the industry at large? The answers to these questions frame the thinking of the leader, and thinking drives behaviors and ultimately the results you achieve on the job. In my work I've observed four mindset stages. Each represents an important shift in thinking. My job is to help leaders recognize when they are on the cusp of another stage and guide them to the next level.

Stage-One Mindset—Self

Early in their careers, leaders start by focusing on self. It may seem obvious, but there are a few important developmental insights that occur before folks can begin thinking of themselves as leaders. The first is the shift from having a "job" to having a career. In the beginning, employees often view a job as a means to an end. *I need a job to have spending money or to buy my first car. I need a job to save money for college.* Or *I need a job so I can afford to live on my own.* Although the time varies from person to person, at some point employees realize that they will be working for a long time. They shift from being grateful to have a job to understanding they have a choice. At this stage of development, it is important to pose questions that help colleagues discover the environment that they both enjoy and thrive in.

I use a conjoint analysis technique, a method of comparing and choosing between a pair of options, to surface the unconscious choices we make when we take a job. I ask clients not to overthink their answers; the magic comes when looking across answers for patterns. I ask them to choose which they prefer:

Do You Prefer Option A. . .	or	Do You Prefer Option B?
Large Company	or	Small Company
Large Company	or	Midsized Company
Small Company	or	Midsized Company
Work Outdoors	or	Work Indoors
Work in an Office	or	Work at Home
Work Days	or	Work Nights
Work Only Mon–Fri	or	Willing to Work Weekends

Do You Prefer Option A. . .	or	Do You Prefer Option B?
Work Alone	or	Work on a Team
Live in the Northeast	or	Live in the Southeast
Live in the West	or	Live in the East
Live in the Midwest	or	Live in the South
Work in a Field Office	or	Work at Corporate Headquarters
Work in Sales	or	Work in Finance
Work in Operations	or	Work in Marketing
Work in a Technical Field	or	Work in a Non-Technical Field
Work on Paper	or	Work on a Computer
Work with People Who Have the Same Background and Knowledge as You Do	or	Work with People Who Have Different Backgrounds and Knowledge Than You Do

I could go on, but you get the picture. You have choice when it comes to work, and happier, more successful employees make those choices consciously. We are more likely to win the races we choose to run and lose races that others choose for us. Wanting to work in a large, Northeastern technical company as a functional member of a functional team is very different than working in a small company, outdoors in the South. Knowing the difference helps you plan your career.

The second shift I observe during this stage is viewing the job as a profession and yourself as a professional. When a job has the environmental characteristics that they want, I observe employees beginning to see their role as a profession. With this mindset shift, the self begins to build a personal brand and connect with the larger community of colleagues who have chosen the same profession. At this point, the supervisor or mentor's role is to nurture a sense of pride by training coworkers to higher levels of job performance and encouraging them to get formal qualifications if appropriate. Development focuses on performing well on the job and learning how others have grown to take on roles of increased complexity and responsibility over time. Mentors are important at this stage of development to guide mentees as they struggle to gain technical knowledge and build role-specific skills.

The third shift I see at this stage, and the first sign of leadership potential, is the realization that leaders need good followers. You can't be a leader if no one is following you. Many workers at this stage do not make this connection. They make a clear distinction between leaders and followers, or management and employees. They see the world as two camps that at best understand their roles and do their jobs, and at worst, distrust each other. Employees who don't make this third shift can still be leaders, delivering results in their role and helping others become good at their craft, but their mindset will limit them in the long run.

Those with higher leadership potential want to be good followers. They want to do a good job, but they believe if they help their bosses achieve their goals by doing good work, then they too will be recognized and rewarded by being promoted and given increased responsibility. They begin to see managers not as a separate group of coworkers to be avoided, but as role models who should be observed, studied, and emulated.

Up to this point, focus and energy have been on the self. We see the beginning of a broader awareness as workers look to learn from bosses, but the motivation is still to promote the self. The image of the self grows and expands to become part of a larger group at stage two.

Stage-Two Mindset—Department/Function

At the next mindset stage, leaders focus on their department and/or function. At this point leaders have succeeded by performing well on the job, getting promoted, and building strong relationships within their area. The majority of colleagues I've worked with stay in this stage-two mindset. They remain at this stage because of the natural laws of community and a clear path to success.

Humans are social beings and there are natural limits to communities. The British anthropologist and evolutionary psychologist Robin Dunbar suggested that there's an effective limit to the number of coherent, face-to-face relationships that a person can sustain. Dunbar used the average human brain size and extrapolated from the results of

primates that humans can comfortably maintain only 150 stable relationships.[5] "Dunbar's number," or 150 people, was about the limit at
which human societies could regulate themselves on the basis of relationships rather than the need for rules and hierarchy.[6] People tend to
organize themselves in groups of a particular size:

- **Teams:** Three to six people represent a nuclear family, close
  friendship group, or a Special Forces team.
- **Groups:** Ten to fifteen people represent an extended friendship
  group, a squad in the military, or a project group.
- **Community:** Around fifty people represent a platoon in the military or a department.
- **Network:** Approximately 150 people represent the size of a clan
  or a company in the military.[7]

While researchers continue to debate Dunbar's findings, the point
is to recognize the importance of teams, groups, communities, and networks of people, and the influence they have over getting things accomplished. Humans are social creatures, and it is important to plug into the
networks of people that have influence with the larger social structure.
The explosion of social media leads society to believe that technology
can expand our communities if they are online, but closer examination
refutes that assumption. Jakob Nielsen, a usability guru, says that in any
online community, 90 percent of people are "lurkers" who just visit and
read others' contributions, 9 percent sometimes contribute, and 1 percent
accounts for most contributions in the community.[8]

The majority of development and the biggest influencers of your
mindset are your immediate team, group, community, and network.
The longer we remain in a given role and department, the more we tend
to protect that group by focusing on its long-term survival and sustain-
ability. Over time we view all actions and decisions through our department lens. Is this project good for our team? Will that new product or
service help or hurt our group in the long run? If this leader is the new
CEO, how will it affect our department?

The other reason we remain loyal to the group is career success.
Performing at a high level while remaining loyal to your community
is one of the fastest and safest ways to get promoted. It is a smoother

path to rise through the ranks of a single area, say finance, marketing, or sales, than it is to move laterally, taking roles in finance, then marketing. Each time you move, you become an outsider that must build relationships in a new community.

To break down these barriers and encourage employees to grow, senior leaders force cross-pollination using special projects, rotational leadership development programs, lateral moves, and job swapping.

Despite the appeal of remaining at stage two, some brave leaders are willing to go to the next level, and when they do, a whole new world opens up.

Stage-Three Mindset—Enterprise

When you hear about surveys, or read articles and books talking about the lack of leadership or the need for more leaders, what they are talking about is the stage-three enterprise mindset. Organizations need leaders who can think strategically, build high-performing teams, work across boundaries, and drive innovation and change. That requires leaving the comfort and safety of the stage-two mindset and adopting an enterprise mindset. You can't build an effective strategy that maximizes only one department, product, or company location. Building high-performing teams is difficult if your network is limited to one area. Working across boundaries will seem impossible if you have not built a broad community that touches the major parts of the companies' operations and corporate functions. Innovation and change are team sports that require trust, resources, and buy-in from across the organization.

In my experience, the majority of leaders promoted from within an organization that fail do so because they have trouble or are unable to adopt an enterprise mindset. Like learning a foreign language, the younger you try to adopt the enterprise mindset, the easier it is. Based on this observation, I try to plant this seed early in people's careers.

Sara was a bright young actuary when she was selected to be part of the enterprise leadership development program. The program is designed to prepare high-potential employees with three to seven years of experience for key leadership roles and a path to senior leadership. Participants are given four six-month rotations. The goal is to create agile leaders with broad exposure to our various businesses. Sara aspires to be the president of an organization one day. She has the ability, drive, and determination to succeed, so I thought it important to plant the enterprise mindset seed early. We were walking together down the central corridor in our Hartford, Connecticut, building one day. The halls were filled with workers on the way to the cafeteria. I turned to Sara and said, "What do you see?"

She said, "People."

"What else?" I prompted.

"People getting food, employees?" she replied in a questioning voice.

"This is what I see. I see people trying to get ahead in their career. I see people trying to buy their first house or pay their mortgage. I see parents with kids in college or trying to get into college and wondering how they are going to pay for it," I told her. "If you want to be president one day, then you have to see these things. Your actions and your decisions will decide if these people can buy a house, or what type of house they can afford. Your actions will determine if they can send their kids to a public school or a private school. Whether these people get to keep their job will depend on your ability to learn to grow and develop as a leader."

I've given this type of talk to many employees. I just let the words stand and most colleagues are silent afterward. Though few ever mention the conversation again, Sara was different. When Sara graduated from the program, she took a director job in our field operation. I ran into her in the hallway, and she said managing employees and being a leader was more involved then she first thought. A member of her team had passed away unexpectedly, and her team asked her what they should do.

"People wanted to know if the team should send flowers and attend the funeral. In that moment I realized I was responsible for everyone. I remembered what you said to me in the hallway." Sara is on her way to becoming an effective leader.

Stage-Four Mindset—Industry/World

The final mindset shift occurs when people begin to think about their actions in the broadest sense. *How do my actions affect my industry and the world as a whole? Is my work not only helping my organization succeed but contributing to the image society has of my industry, and do my actions positively impact the world?* CEOs often refer to this as the triple bottom line—a framework or theory that recommends that companies commit to focus on social and environmental concerns just as they do on profits. The idea is that we can manage a company in a way that not only earns financial profits, but which also improves people's lives and the planet.[9]

Over the past ten years, my mindset has shifted from a stage-three enterprise mindset to a stage-four world mindset. When I joined Aetna's enterprise strategy department, my focus was working across departments to make the organization successful. I wanted to mentor and grow agile leaders who were willing to break down functional silos and make decisions that prioritized company success over their department's success. When Aetna's CEO Mark Bertolini and Chief Human Resources Officer Elease Wright moved me from strategy to human resources, they expanded my leadership lens. Over the past ten years I've seen the importance of taking a world view. Many organizations and executives limit their investment in employees and leaders because they don't see an immediate return on that investment. I can't tell you how often someone has said to me, "Why should I spend the time and money training workers? They just leave and go to a competitor."

I did not have a good answer for that question when I had a stage-three enterprise mindset. But I do with a stage-four world mindset. We have a responsibility to society and the world to develop competent, inspiring, successful leaders. The world needs good leaders. If I train and grow a good leader who leaves my organization, the world is better off and so is my organization because that person will remember the investment we made in their future. If I inherit a poorly trained leader, then my organization and the world is worse off.

As an economics major, I learned Gresham's Law, the monetary principle that "bad money drives out good." Imagine there are two types of dimes in circulation, each accepted as being worth ten cents. One is made of 100 percent silver and another is made of 90 percent silver and 10 percent copper. Over time, the 100 percent silver coins will disappear as people realize they can make a cheaper coin that has the same value. If we don't take a world view on leadership development, we inadvertently create a race to the bottom and invest fewer resources and less time to create good leaders.

Belief/Behavior

The second component of the leader success journey is the belief/behavior link. As leaders develop, they become aware of the link, better understand the link, and then consciously control the link.

Awareness

First, leaders must become aware of the link. In 1952, Norman Vincent Peale published the bestselling book *The Power of Positive Thinking*. It promoted the link between our thinking, our behavior, and the results we achieve in life. The last sixty years have seen a dramatic increase in research and interest in positive psychology, neuroscience, well-being, and mindfulness. Bestselling books like *The Secret* by Rhonda Byrne and *The Power of Now* by Eckhart Tolle are examples of this trend reaching a mainstream and global audience. These and other writings highlight the law of attraction and how it manifests through our thoughts. "Like attracts like" and "we attract into our life whatever we focus on" represent core principles.

Based on the understanding of the power of our thoughts, people have used various strategies like creative visualization, affirmations, meditation, and mindfulness practices to gain inner peace and achieve desired outcomes.

In my work it does not matter whether the spiritual, personal, or business path led leaders to become aware of the link; what is important is they are now aware it exists. As the comedian Eddie Griffin said, "Christians say Jesus is the message, the Muslims say it is Muhammad . . . I say, did you get the message?"[10]

Understanding and Controlling the Link

Good leaders understand that their beliefs drive their behavior and ultimately, outcomes. Brain science also confirms this link. Charles Jacobs, author of *Management Rewired: Why Feedback Doesn't Work and Other Surprising Lessons from the Latest Brain Science*, serves as a business advisor helping me develop senior leaders. He helps leaders understand that we live in a world of our own creation, and we make decisions emotionally and justify them with logic. Smart leaders craft and communicate powerful stories that link belief and behavior.

Stories are thoughts wrapped in emotion. A story is a lens to view the world and a lever to transform it. Charles shares that all great leaders tell an aspirational story with a transformation at the end. Think of Rev. Dr. Martin Luther King's "I have a dream" speech or President John F. Kennedy's "We will send a man to the moon and back" speech.

Over time, leaders learn that an aspirational narrative ensures everyone knows what to do in every situation, and it fills in the details that business plans leave out. In Charles's words:[11]

> The story the organization tells itself is its culture . . . The best leaders make it a priority to shape it . . . We are the stories we tell ourselves and over time what we say to ourselves becomes embedded into our neuro networks . . . What is real is the story we choose to tell ourselves.

Just like the mindset component, where leaders adopt a broader perspective lens, leaders create a stronger belief/behavior link using intentional, well-crafted stories. These aspirational narratives describe where they want to take an organization and inspire people to action.

Success Formula

Success formula, the final component of the leader's journey, is an approach or system that develops over a long period of time (fifteen-plus years) that reflects your mindset, values, beliefs, and past success. It distills the wisdom you've accumulated and puts it into a form that can be shared and emulated by others. Let's look at a couple of examples to better understand the concept.

W. Edwards Deming's Fourteen Points

Deming was an electrical engineer and statistician who helped develop the sampling techniques used by the US Department of the Census and the Bureau of Labor Statistics. In the 1950s, Deming was brought to

Japan at the request of General Douglas MacArthur to help plan for the 1951 Japanese Census and help revive Japan's shattered postwar economy.

While in Japan, Deming shared his expertise in quality-control techniques and trained hundreds of engineers, managers, and scholars in statistical process control. He also conducted a session with top management including Akio Morita, the cofounder of Sony Corp. Deming's message to Japan's chief executives was that improving quality would reduce expenses, while increasing productivity and market share.[12]

A number of Japanese manufacturers applied his techniques widely and experienced heretofore unheard-of levels of quality and productivity. The improved quality combined with the lowered cost created new international demand for Japanese products. To repay him for his friendship and kindness, Japan created the Deming Prize and in 1960, awarded Deming Japan's Order of the Sacred Treasure, Second Class.[13]

Deming over a number of years created and refined his success formula. We know it today as the fourteen points of total quality management:

1. Create constancy of purpose for improving products and services.
2. Adopt the new philosophy.
3. Cease dependence on inspection to achieve quality.
4. End the practice of awarding business on price alone; instead, minimize total cost by working with a single supplier.
5. Improve constantly and forever every process for planning, production, and service.
6. Institute training on the job.
7. Adopt and institute leadership.
8. Drive out fear.
9. Break down barriers between staff areas.
10. Eliminate slogans, exhortations, and targets for the workforce.
11. Eliminate numerical quotas for the workforce and numerical goals for management.
12. Remove barriers that rob people of pride of workmanship and eliminate the annual rating or merit system.
13. Institute a vigorous program of education and self-improvement for everyone.
14. Put everybody in the company to work accomplishing the transformation.

John Wooden's Pyramid of Success

Wooden is considered the greatest basketball coach of all time. He is one of only three men enshrined in the Basketball Hall of Fame as both a player and as a coach (Bill Sharman and Lenny Wilkens are the others). He led Purdue to the 1932 national championship as a player. As a coach of Indiana State Teachers College in 1947–48, he won the conference title but turned down an invitation to participate in the postseason tournament because it did not allow African Americans to compete. Within days, the National Association of Intercollegiate Basketball (NAIB) changed its policy, and Coach Wooden accepted the tournament invitation.[14]

Figure 5.2. John Wooden's Pyramid of Success

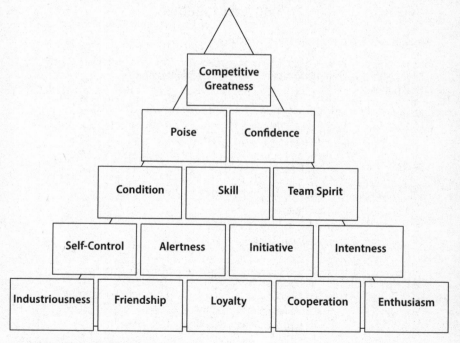

Adapted from coachwooden.com.

In 1949, Coach Wooden took over the UCLA basketball program, and over the next twenty-six years won ten national championships. He received the Presidential Medal of Freedom in ceremonies at the White House, the highest civilian honor America gives.[15]

Over his professional career, Coach Wooden wrote several books and honed his philosophy on leadership. He spent years speaking to business and sports audiences, sharing his views. His success formula, the Pyramid of Success, highlights fifteen values—including friendship, self-control, team spirit, poise, and competitive greatness (see figure 5.2). He also describes twelve important leadership lessons, including: a) good values attract good people; b) make each day your masterpiece; and c) adversity is your asset. Visit www.coachwooden.com/pyramid-of-success to see John Wooden's entire system.

Putting It All Together

Worksheet 5: Leader Success Journey

Leadership Component	Key Question	Working Assumption
Mindset	Where is your primary focus: self, department, enterprise, or world?	
Belief/Behavior	Describe your two or three most important leadership beliefs.	
Success Formula	What approach has allowed you to be successful in the past?	

Successful leaders expand their mindset, deepen their understanding of the belief/behavior link, and create a unique success formula. As they mature, they realize they don't directly change the colleagues they lead. Instead, the leader changes first, which in turn affects others. Intuitively we know this, but it is difficult to do in practice. You can't make someone trust you, but if you are trustworthy, people will grow to trust you.

Use worksheet 5 to sketch out your leader success journey. Revisit and update it as often as you need. There is great power in writing your views on paper. If you are not sure about a particular component, write your hypothesis or best guess.

My Leadership-Development Success Formula

Earlier in this chapter, I told you how my primary focus shifted from a stage-three enterprise mindset to a stage-four world mindset. My success formula is based on my belief that the ability to describe your leadership style in a clear way to others—employers, employees, team members, friends, and family—is important. Since you can't get by in this world without several people asking you about your leadership, it is important to know what to say. So, let's start with my two core principles (what I'd describe as Belief/Behavior in worksheet 5).

Belief/Behavior Principle #1: Think of leadership as a verb and not a noun. It's active, something you can do, not an immutable quality you have. Leadership involves *moving* an organization, process, and/or idea from Point A to Point B. When you are taking actions to move forward, you are leading. If you are not, then you are not leading. Therefore, leadership is not something you "achieve" via a title. Since leadership is a set of actions, then anyone can lead, which brings us to the second principle.

Belief/Behavior Principle #2: Congratulations, everyone is a leader! Principle #2 should take the pressure off you worrying about how to be a leader, and instead focus you on better describing how you lead—how you act to move something from Point A to Point B. In my experience, the better you are at communicating how you lead, the easier it will be for you to identify the right job opportunities, build better teams, and set yourself up for success.

Every year it is a good practice to review the successes you've had and ask yourself what approach allowed you to be successful. The goal is to identify these behaviors, patterns, and approaches. This input becomes the starting point for creating your success formula.

Identify Your Leadership Preferences

I created an assessment to help clients identify their leadership preference. I use the term "preference" or "style" instead of "type" because how you lead can be situational and flexible, but we tend to have primary and secondary approaches.

The concept of Leadership Preferences that I developed focuses on thinking and behavior, and how that thinking is communicated to others to accomplish personal and organizational goals. Better understanding of personal preferences can be used to build more effective teams. You naturally will attract people who are like you. The goal is to have enough self-awareness to know who you are, so you can get coworkers on your team who complement your leadership style.

I am presenting just one of many ways to understand your leadership style. I do not claim that my way is the best method for everyone. My clients find my method useful because it gives them simple, relevant language for how they can add value to an organization. The goal is to use any method that gives you true insight and understanding for how you behave and how that behavior affects other workers as you try to accomplish goals. (At the end of this section, I describe other popular methods you can use.)

Leadership Preferences is based upon a person's view of their organization and its relationship to its marketplace. Some employees view their organization in terms of its potential to achieve a vision or fulfill a mission. Others see their organization as a way to fulfill the needs of customers in the marketplace. Some view their organization as a set of policies, processes, and people, designed as a system to deliver products and services in a predictable and efficient manner. Others see their organization as a collection of employees working together to grow and develop. All views are valid and needed to ensure organizational success.

In my work I have found that the views described above translate into four basic leadership preferences—vision-centered leaders, customer-centered leaders, organization-centered leaders, and people-centered leaders.

The Leadership Preferences Survey is located in appendix A of this book and online at tedfleming.com. To get the most out of this chapter, complete the assessment, either in this book or online. Then come back to better understand your results and how you can use that information to develop your career, build your team, and accomplish your goals.

Interpreting Your Scores

The total score across the four preferences should equal 200. If not, please review the scoring of your answers. Understanding your scores:

- 65 or Greater: This means you almost exclusively use this leadership style in a given situation.
- 60 to 64: You have a strong preference for using this leadership style.
- 55 to 59: You have a moderate preference for using this leadership style.
- 46 to 54: You may or may not use this leadership style depending upon the situation.
- 41 to 45: You have a moderate disregard for using this leadership style.
- 36 to 40: You have a strong disregard for using this leadership style.
- 35 or Less: You virtually neglect using this leadership style.

Each preference has its own strengths and weaknesses. Most people have a single strong preference. Some employees have a combination of preferences. Since no one person can be strong in all four preferences, the goal is to build teams that draw upon the strengths of all four preferences while compensating for the weaknesses of each. Let's explore each style.

Vision-Centered Leaders

A vision-centered leader's core belief is developing new ideas, products, and services in the best way to move an organization forward. He or she leads by creating and communicating a compelling vision of where they wish to take an organization or group (see figure 5.3).

Figure 5.3. Leadership Preferences—The Vision-Centered Leader Lens

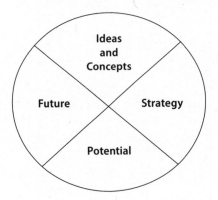

The strengths of a vision-centered leader are the ability to create new ideas, concepts, products, and services by making connections among previously unrelated notions. These leaders focus on the strategy, possibilities, and potential of a group or organization. They have broad knowledge and perspective and are future oriented.

Because of their focus on the future, vision-centered leaders may not be patient enough to focus on the day-to-day details of a task or operation. Often, their ideas can be too complex or theoretical for others to understand. Coworkers will perceive them as loners and/or not good team players.

I believe Richard Branson and Elon Musk are vision-centered leaders because they focus on the future and push the boundaries of what is possible. In Branson's case, he was successful with his airline, Virgin Atlantic, but he expanded into entertainment and aerospace. Musk's success started with electric cars and also migrated to space travel.

Customer-Centered Leaders

A customer-centered leader's core belief is that understanding and meeting customer needs is the best way to move an organization forward. He or she leads by focusing on customers and their problems (see figure 5.4).

Figure 5.4. Leadership Preferences—The Customer-Centered Leader Lens

The strength of a customer-centered leader is the ability to see how trends will affect the current marketplace. They can translate firsthand customer information into products and services that add value. Customer-centered leaders are good relationship managers and excellent problem solvers. They are present oriented.

Because of their focus, customer-centered leaders may be too willing to change to satisfy customers, causing internal turmoil. They may not concentrate on operational efficiency or adhere to organizational policies. Being oriented toward the present, they also might miss breakthrough innovations and trends.

I believe Sara Blakely and Scott Cook are customer-centered leaders because they tend to focus on delivering practical value to customers in competitive environments. In Blakely's case, her Spanx organization manufactures shaping underwear for women and men that helps them look thinner. Cook's Intuit company provides financial, accounting, and tax-support software to individuals and businesses.

Organization-Centered Leaders

An organization-centered leader's core belief is that building a predictable and repeatable system for delivering products and services is the best way to move an organization forward. He or she leads by focusing on internal processes, policies, and procedures (see figure 5.5).

Figure 5.5. Leadership Preferences—The Organization-Centered Leader Lens

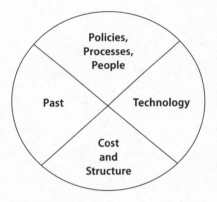

The strengths of an organization-centered leader are the ability to organize people and their work to get things done. They can translate people, policies, and processes into products and services that add value. Organization-centered leaders are excellent negotiators and know how to build effective teams. They can maneuver through complex, large political organizations effectively. They are past oriented, i.e., they focus on what has worked in the past and how to apply that to the present.

Because of their internal and detailed focus, organization-centered leaders may have trouble explaining the big picture or vision. They might not treat others as unique individuals, instead always focusing on the team. Also, they might not be the best people to lead an organization during a crisis or when quick, decisive action is called for.

I think Ursula Burns and Ray Kroc are examples of organization-centered leadership because they made large, complex organizations more efficient and effective. Burns was the first African American woman to head a Fortune 500 company—Xerox. She is often quoted as saying, "No fancy words, bold bets, and back to basics." Kroc is famous for the explosive growth of McDonald's by focusing on consistent, reliable, repeatable service and operations.

People-Centered Leaders

A people-centered leader's core belief is that developing people and providing them with opportunities to shine is the best way to move an organization forward. He or she leads by developing the people who work around them (see figure 5.6).

Figure 5.6. Leadership Preferences— The People-Centered Leader Lens

The greatest strength of a people-centered leader is the ability to translate employee potential into products and services that add value. People-centered leaders are good judges of talent and excellent mentors. They can create climates where employees want to do their best. They empower others. People-centered leaders are present oriented, i.e., they focus on what they can do in the present that will prepare employees for the future.

People-centered leaders may focus on the few with talent, while neglecting other members of the team. They may be overly optimistic about people's motivation and desire to improve. Subordinates might see them as too critical, or as leaders that take too long to make decisions.

I believe Jaime Escalante and Shonda Rhimes are people-centered leaders because they focus on coaching and developing those around them as the path to success. Escalante was a famous educator known for teaching calculus at Garfield High School in East Los Angeles. He proved that inner-city students could excel given the right support. Rhimes guides teams of writers and production staff to create television shows like *Grey's Anatomy*, *Private Practice*, and *Scandal*.

Flat-Profile Leaders

While most people have a strong preference for one style, there are a few who show no single strong preference. I call these people flat-profile leaders. The strengths of a flat-profile leader are the ability to be flexible and adaptable. If the leader can recognize the type of leadership style that would be most effective in a given situation, she or he has the ability to mirror that style.

The downside of a flat-profile leader is difficulty building an effective team or inner circle. Having a strong leadership preference makes it easier to see your deficiencies and pick leaders who are strong where you are weak. The other potential problem is effectively communicating which style you are employing at a given time. The risk is that others working with you will think your style is inconsistent. Team members might have a hard time deciphering your true desires.

Combinations

Some people have a single strong preference and one other moderate or strong preference. Those with a combination of preferences bring strong and unique abilities to their leadership role. Understanding these distinct abilities is key to building an effective inner circle or senior management team.

Vision/Customer Combination (VC)

Characteristics of the VC leadership combination are a broad, strategic view and the ability to solve customer problems. This combination is ideally suited for entrepreneurs.

A vision-centered leader sees more than others see, sees farther than others see, and sees before others do. The VC leader uses this ability to develop creative solutions to business problems. A customer-centered leader becomes an expert at understanding their customers' business. They use this deep customer knowledge to create products and services that will meet customers' current and unrecognized needs.

VC leaders are uniquely able to be good entrepreneurs because they concretely marry their ability to anticipate future trends and insights with specific customer needs. In other words, they naturally see the creation of new market space.

Organization/Vision Combination (OV)

Characteristics of the OV leadership combination are the ability to organize people and their activities with a broad, strategic view of the organization. This combination is ideally suited for CEOs and senior leaders of large organizations.

Organization-centered leaders are good at getting things done. They are good process managers who know how to build infrastructures that deliver reliable, durable, and most of all, repeatable products and services. They are usually adept at integrating technology into an organization. A vision-centered leader sees more than others see, sees farther than others see, and sees before others do. The OV leader uses this ability to build teams that are adept at implementing strategies.

OV leaders are uniquely able to run large organizations because of their ability to maneuver through complex and political environments. They can focus both externally on the marketplace and internally on operations. Having vision along with organizational skill as a preference is significant because it reduces one of the major weaknesses of the organizational style, namely the inability to create and explain the big picture.

In short, the OV leader can determine where the organization needs to go and then chart a course to get there.

People/Vision Combination (PV)

Characteristics of the PV leadership combination are the ability to get the best out of people and a broad, strategic view of the organization. This combination is ideally suited for coaches, teachers, or mentors.

A people-centered leader is good at recognizing talent. She and he are excellent mentors and know how to create climates where employees want to do their best. A vision-centered leader sees more than others see, sees farther than others see, and sees before others do. The PV leader uses this ability to develop colleagues to fill key roles in the organization.

PV leaders are good coaches because they can push people to their physical and creative limits. They are aware of people's dreams and goals and are eager to share ownership. With an emphasis on vision and personnel, PV leaders can develop employees in line with the strategic direction of the organization. That makes this combination an attractive head of human resources for a rapidly growing company. This person could also serve as the nontechnical leader of a highly technical project team.

Customer/People Combination (CP)

Characteristics of the CP leadership combination are the ability to solve customer problems and getting the best out of employees. This combination is ideally suited for sales and marketing professionals.

A customer-centered leader becomes an expert at understanding her or his customers' business. They use this deep customer knowledge to create products and services that will meet customers' current and unrecognized needs. A people-centered leader is good at predicting behavior in any given situation and developing staff. The CP leader uses this ability to be the "eyes and ears" of the organization in the marketplace. They can provide insight on how the organization's products and services are perceived by current and potential customers.

CP leaders are good sales and marketing professionals because they can build effective long-term relationships with customers. Their people skills allow them to recognize both the stated and unstated needs of customers. Then they can effectively communicate these business requirements to internal staff.

Organization/People Combination (OP)

Characteristics of the OP leadership combination are the ability to organize workers and the ability to get the best from them. This combination is ideally suited for project managers and chiefs of staff.

An organization-centered leader is good at getting things done. They are good process managers that know how to build infrastructures to deliver reliable, durable, and repeatable products and services. They are usually adept at integrating technology into an organization. A people-centered leader is good at predicting staffers' behavior in any given situation and recognizing talent. They are excellent mentors and know how to create climates where people want to do their best.

OP leaders are good project managers because they can assemble effective teams. They can recognize talent, develop people's skills, and organize their activities to implement a strategy or tactic. An OP's ability to maneuver through political environments makes them uniquely qualified to manage complex projects in large organizations. They keep all employees focused on the end goal. They are the ultimate "can-do" leaders.

Customer/Organization Combination (CO)

Characteristics of the CO leadership combination are the ability to solve customer problems and the ability to organize people and their activities. This combination is ideally suited for operations management.

A customer-centered leader becomes an expert at understanding their customers' business. An organization-centered leader knows how to build infrastructures that deliver reliable, durable, and repeatable products and services.

CO leaders are uniquely suited for operations management because of their ability to translate firsthand customer information into desirable products and services. Further, they are able to create policies and processes, and build the internal teams to deliver the proposed products and services in a cost-effective manner.

How to Apply Leadership Preferences Insights

Information from the Leadership Preferences Survey can be used for development, for improving the effectiveness of communication, and for understanding the culture of an organization. Applications include:

Development. Knowing your preferences allows you to develop in two ways. Imagine you are a vision-centered leader. First, you can find a mentor with the same preference, but who operates at a higher level. If you are a midlevel manager, a senior manager that uses the same style can show you how to effectively deploy that style in more complex environments. The person can serve as a role model for what is possible. Second, you can find a mentor who can point out and address your potential blind spots. In this example, an organization-centered leader can help you translate your vision into a reality. The model is also useful for the development of leadership teams. Accurate assessment of employees' leadership preferences aids the organization by identifying its strengths and gaps. It can provide a profile of the attributes the team needs to become more effective.

Communication. Understanding the preferences of those around you allows a leader to translate strategies, tactics, and messages into a language that others can understand, which improves the overall effectiveness of communication. As mentioned before, most employers are looking for leaders and leadership skills. Use the language associated with each style to describe what type of leadership you would bring to the role. Imagine a computer salesperson who is a customer-centered leader trying to get a management role in a household-products manufacturing firm. Although the customer-centered leader would not seem like a fit for the organization-leader-dominated firm, the customer-centered leader would highlight how their deep understanding of customer needs would enable them to develop products and services that generate profit and identify new market space. Working with traditional organization insiders would ensure products were produced with high quality, on time and on budget.

Culture. Profiling an entire organization or sub-unit identifies whether the culture is internally or externally focused. It also highlights whether an organization emphasizes the people or the process. With this knowledge, you can introduce people, values, and beliefs to focus the culture to achieve results. Imagine an energy-consulting firm loaded with customer- and people-centered leaders. Traditionally, consulting firms are loaded with customer-centric employees who are skilled at questioning clients to determine what solutions will work best. They usually have good people leaders that recognize talent. But customer and people leaders tend to focus on the present. Understanding the dominant culture allows leadership to consciously hire vision leaders who focus on what the consulting firm will need to do in the future to grow, and organization leaders who will identify what has worked well for clients in the past.

As I mentioned before, Leadership Preferences is one of many methods. Two other popular and respected assessments are the Myers/Briggs Type Indicator and DiSC Profile.

According to the sixth edition of the Myers/Briggs Type Indicator (MBTI), MBTI helps people understand their psychological type.[16] Based upon the theory of personality developed by Carl Jung, it identifies the differences in behavior resulting from inborn tendencies for humans to use their minds in different ways. There are sixteen combinations, or types, based upon two opposite ways people perceive information—sensing and intuition—and two opposite ways people judge—thinking and feeling. Finally, Jung noted that people tend to focus their energy and be energized more by the external world of others, experience, and activity or the internal world of ideas, memories, and emotions. MBTI calls these two orientations extraversion (focus on outer world) and introversion (focus on the inner world).

Another popular psychological tool is the DiSC Profile. Based upon the work of William Moulton Marston, it assesses people along two opposite perceptions, the degree to which a person feels more or less powerful than their environment, and the degree to which a person sees the environment as favorable or unfavorable.[17] Behavior is based upon the following four primary dimensions:

- Dominance: Direct and Decisive
- Influence: Optimistic and Outgoing
- Steadiness: Sympathetic and Cooperative
- Conscientiousness: Concerned and Correct

No matter which assessment methods or tools you use, at the end of the process you want to have a good idea of your skills and leadership style.

Figure 5.7. Leadership Preferences—Core Leadership Preferences: Definitions

Leadership Preference	Defined
Vision Centered	Vision-centered leaders create and communicate a compelling vision of where they wish to take an organization or group. They come up with new ideas, concepts, products, and services by making connections among previously unrelated notions.
Customer Centered	Customer-centered leaders focus on customers and their problems. They are able to translate firsthand customer information into products and services that add value.
Organization Centered	Organization-centered leaders organize people and their activities to get things done. They are able to translate people, policies, and processes into products and services that add value.
People Centered	People-centered leaders develop the staff members that work with them. They are able to translate employee potential into products and services that add value.

■ ■ ■

Leadership is becoming a universal skill required at all levels of organizations. The need is compounded by the flattening of organizational structures and the use of technology to create distributed and diverse workforces. It is getting rarer for a manager to both be in the same physical location as her team and be able to oversee all the work of the team. Individuals, groups, and departments are asked to self-govern to achieve their desired results.

That means everyone is a leader. You must recognize and communicate what type of leader you are, along with its strengths and gaps. Your approach for moving an organization forward is important. Use the Leadership Preferences Survey to uncover which one of the four leadership archetypes you are: vision, customer, organization, and people. You can use this information to build strong, diverse teams that link you to business results:

- Vision-centered leaders are your link to competitive advantage; they keep you one step ahead of the competition by focusing on the future and what is possible.
- Customer-centered leaders link you to top-line or revenue growth; they ensure your products and services address a current need that will generate sales.
- Organization-centered leaders link you to bottom-line growth; they add processes and systems that generate profit.
- People-centered leaders allow you to implement the vision and deliver on your promises by identifying and developing your most important resource—your personnel.

Bottom line: Think of leadership as a "verb"
and not a "noun"; it's a team sport.

Armed with an understanding of how to develop their mindset, beliefs, and success formula, and how to articulate their leadership style, staff members are ready to climb to the top of the corporate ladder. I see many colleagues who work hard to achieve their goals, but winning is a team sport, so who else is working hard for you? Getting others to work on your behalf is important, and it starts with cultivating your image, as you'll see in the next chapter.

CHAPTER 6

Spheres of Influence: Cultivate Your Image

Image is everything.

—Andre Agassi

A ndre Agassi said these words in a 1991 television ad for the Canon EOS Rebel camera. It featured Andre hitting tennis balls, wearing fashionable clothes, and driving cool cars. He got a lot of flak for that commercial, with many questioning if he was serious about tennis. Now, image may not be *everything*, but it is extremely important if you want to get ahead in your career.

In the hit musical *Hamilton*, Lin-Manuel Miranda has a song called "The Room Where It Happens." It discusses the Compromise of 1790 between Alexander Hamilton on one side and Thomas Jefferson and James Madison on the other. Jefferson suggested a dinner where the three could talk. In the end, Hamilton got Jefferson and Madison to agree that the US Treasury would take over and pay state debts, making New York the locus of financial power, while Hamilton agreed to locate the permanent national capital on the Virginia-Maryland border (Washington, DC). Yet our understanding of this important event comes entirely from Jefferson's account of that evening; Miranda's lyrics recount how no one really knows exactly what happened behind closed doors. The Aaron Burr character wants to be in the room where the decisions are being made. He wants to be in the room where it happens.

But the reality is, you are not in the room when it happens for you. Consider the following situations:

- Your boss decides what to give you for a raise, bonus, and/or equity.
- Your boss puts you on his/her succession plan.
- The senior management team decides to promote you.
- You make partner at your firm.
- A company decides to extend you a job offer.
- A client refers your organization or services to another person or company.

In most of these scenarios, you are not in the room where that decision happened. But what is? Your image. Image is what others say about you and how you deliver results. Components of image include the messages you send to others through your dress, voice, attitude, and other visible cues. Some people prefer the word "reputation," but I like the word "image" because it is a "picture" people have of you. People share that picture or perception of you, and that is often the basis of key decisions.

So, what should your image be? Should it change over time? And how do you change your image if you don't like what others say? These are important questions that I will discuss individually. Let's start with what your image should be, and if it should it change over time.

I believe image should evolve over time. Your image should have a strong core that does not change, with other aspects complementing that core. To give the discussion some structure, think of four types of career phases: 1) the early-in-career or individual contributor (an employee who does not have other coworkers reporting to him/her) phase; 2) the manager of individual contributors or manager of managers phase; 3) the executive leader phase; and 4) the entrepreneur phase. During any given career, people move in and out of these four phases.

If you are early in your career or not a manager of employees (i.e., an individual contributor), exceptional performance is the image you want.

Another positive image is "grit" as defined by Angela Duckworth, the cofounder and CEO of Character Lab, and Christopher H. Browne, Distinguished Professor of Psychology at the University of Pennsylvania. Duckworth defines "grit" as the ability to stick with a task in the face of obstacles or perseverance, tenacity, and doggedness.[18] If you are new to an industry, company, or role, having a gritty image serves you well while you are learning the job. As you mature in that role, your image evolves from tenacity to achievement. Another useful core image is adaptability—the skill to quickly learn and adjust to the changing demands of the internal and external environment.

At the manager level, the image you want to portray is possessing senior leader potential. On the performance side, managers generally need a reputation for strategic execution, leading change, and guiding teams. The heart of a manager's job is translating organizational strategy into an operational plan of action to deliver results. To produce those results, you must attract, develop, and retain the talent needed to execute the plan and inspire and engage others to realize the change. But as you go up the corporate ladder, good performance is seen as the price of admission. As Harvey J. Coleman, the author of *Empowering Yourself: The Organizational Game Revealed*, states, "Organizations pay for performance but tend to promote based on potential."[19]

So, your image evolves from one of exceptional performance to high-level potential. What does that look like? One of the core images of potential is insight—the ability to turn information and data into new products, services, processes, and possibilities. Another core image is engagement or connection—the ability to persuasively communicate with people both within your department or area and outside of it. People recognize your ability to connect different parts of the organization together to get things done that could not get done independently. Your influence grows, and people trust you because of this ability.

At the executive-leader level, your image must evolve from potential to demonstrated mastery and executive presence. Think of the executive level as a country club where the members must approve your application. Can colleagues see you at the table? The image centers on soft skills. As Susan Peters, senior vice president of human resources at General Electric, said, "The reasons behind an executive's success or failure rarely relate to technical skills or specific experience. It's almost always the leadership, the soft skills."[20]

Conveying the image of a leader with presence is important but can be vague to many people. One of the best books I've found on the subject is Sylvia Ann Hewlett's *Executive Presence*. In it, she outlines three areas that together make up executive presence. The first is *gravitas*—do you have the image of grace under fire and the ability to make difficult decisions? The second is *communication*—are you viewed as having superior speaking skills and the ability to command a room? The final component is *appearance*—do you have the image of being polished, youthful, and vigorous? Executive presence is a necessary image to get to the highest levels of an organization.[21]

Mastery is the other image—a proven track record of success, leading innovation, and/or change. Often the job of a senior leader is to take the organization in a new direction. That means departing from the status quo and getting employees to act and perform in new ways. Achieving an image as innovative and a change agent means you have mastered the ability to build strong teams, work well with internal and external stakeholders, and drive for results.

Another common career phase is that of entrepreneur. Over the last several years I've had the pleasure of working with Gregg Lichtenstein, PhD, president of Collaborative Strategies, LLC, a consulting firm that specializes in working with entrepreneurs. He states that the difference between an entrepreneur and other managers is the ability to deal with a larger number of unknowns.[22] When thinking about an entrepreneur's image, Gregg highlights the following areas:

- **Insight**—the ability to form novel strategic observations that create competitive advantage
- **Decision-Making**—the ability to make strategic choices under conditions of uncertainty
- **Learning**—the ability to discover what strategic moves are effective
- **Adaptability**—the ability to adjust and improvise based on what is being learned

- **Execution**—the ability to perform within time and resource constraints to generate a return on investment
- **Risk Management**—the ability to manage the trade-offs of innovation

Although you may not excel in all the above areas, crafting your image around these qualities makes it easier to attract employees, investors, and partners. Building entrepreneurial skill allows them to manage businesses at various life stages and levels of complexity. It is important to signal the ability to guide an organization from conception, to start-up mode, through rapid growth and maturity.

So, the four career phases have different opportunities and challenges and therefore require changes to your image for you to be successful in the eyes of others. But what do you do if you don't like your image or you simply want to change it? How do you signal that to others? I tell clients to think about the Three Ps of Image: Picture, Practice, and Perception.

Create a Picture

The first step is to create a visual reference or picture of the image you want to convey. A picture can represent several complex ideas or concepts at once. A person can serve as your image. A colleague can represent the level of achievement you wish to attain, the values you share, or the journey you take. Athletes often have a favorite player they try to emulate. They are aware of their records and statistics and use those as inspiration for surpassing their achievements. Jack Nicklaus won eighteen major professional golf championships. It is considered the most significant record in golf. Tiger Woods, who has fifteen majors, had Jack Nicklaus's records on his wall growing up. Nicklaus gave Woods something to shoot for.

Many investors and business leaders look up to Warren Buffett, the philanthropist and chief executive officer of Berkshire Hathaway. They are attracted to his image as a down-to-earth, self-made billionaire who stuck to a philosophy of value investing. Despite his being worth more than $70 billion, people relate to a man who gets his breakfast at

McDonald's, reads papers instead of typing on a computer, and calls folks on the phone to share ideas.

Mother Teresa is seen as an ideal image of compassion and strength. Born Agnes Gonxha Bojaxhiu in Macedonia, Mother Teresa joined the Sisters of Loreto in India. Between 1931 and 1948, she taught at St. Mary's High School in Calcutta. The suffering and poverty she saw in the community touched her so greatly that she received permission from her superiors to leave the convent school and devote herself to working among the poorest of the poor in the slums of Calcutta. Without much financial support, she started an open-air school for slum children. Volunteers helped grow the mission, and her passion and work allowed her to touch people around the world.[23]

Selecting a picture for your image aspiration is important. It allows you to summarize your values, work approach, and desired results in a concrete way. Communicating or sharing that picture with others begins the process of altering your image. Now that you have the picture, it is important to practice developing and honing your new image.

Sharpen Your Image Through Practice

The second P is Practice. Ronald A. Williams, retired chairman and CEO of Aetna, Inc., has described the concept of the "T-shaped" executive. In describing how to develop as a leader, he said the trunk of the T was your towering strength. The top of the T represents your experiences utilizing that strength. Some leaders fail because they have not developed a towering strength. Others fail because they lack the diversity of experiences necessary to lead an organization.

When advising clients, I start with the trunk and ask, "What do you do better than 85 percent of the population?" The exact percentage is not important. The key is to recognize what you do well and be able to put it into words. The towering strength can also be an aspiration. In that case, you want to identify the experiences and education necessary to develop that strength. To create the top, I ask clients to describe the different jobs, projects, and situations where they have used their strength. Look at the example in figure 6.1.

Figure 6.1. Towering Achievement

Internal Audit	Investor Relations	Accounting Manager	Business Unit CFO	Management Consultant	Financial Planner

Towering Strength:
Financial Management

In this figure, the towering strength is financial management. It signals to others how you can add value to an organization. My clients often want an image of possessing several strengths. They believe highlighting a single strength is limiting. While that conclusion seems logical, data would prove otherwise. When making hiring or promotion decisions or selecting team members, leaders look for towering strengths. A quick scan of job descriptions shows that organizations look for experts with a track record of success in a specific area. They group experience in buckets of three to five years' experience, five to seven years' experience, or ten-plus years' experience.

When making promotion decisions, managers are more likely to hire the "functional" expert with direct experience doing the job for a long period of time over the person with a more diverse background. It does not mean you can't get a job without a ton of direct experience (I'll cover that in chapter 8), but it is not the norm.

Finally, while research shows that diverse teams outperform homogeneous teams in the long run, those teams are often comprised of functional experts with towering strengths working on cross-functional teams. Each person uses their strength to provide a unique perspective and the ability to get things done. So, I encourage clients to communicate a towering strength as they craft their image.[24]

The top of the T is where you highlight your diversity of experiences. In the example in figure 6.1, the candidate might say they led a ten-person internal auditing team for a midsized organization. Then they worked in investor relations for a Fortune 500 organization. They started their career as an accounting manager. They worked as a management consultant for a big-four accounting firm and then were recruited to become the business unit CFO for another Fortune 500 company. In their off hours, they provide financial planning services for a nonprofit organization. You differentiate yourself from others with the same towering strength—financial management—by telling stories of how you have applied your strengths in different situations. Job candidates often seem similar until they share their unique experiences.

I advise my clients to look for and imagine situations in which they are the best choice when you couple their strength with their set of experiences. Like generating creative ideas, the perceived limitation of focusing on a single strength instead of many strengths helps focus the mind and expand the number of possibilities. With a picture of the image you want, and practice developing your related core strength, the final step is to help mold the perception others have of you through word branding.

Manage Your Perception

The final P of image after Picture and Practice is Perception. In their book *The 22 Immutable Laws of Branding,* Al and Laura Ries talk about the Law of the Word: a brand should strive to own a word in the mind of the consumer. Once a word is precisely associated with a brand, it is almost impossible for a competitor to create some stronger associations. If you want to build a brand, you must focus your branding efforts on owning a word in the prospect's mind.[25] In workshops I often use luxury cars to demonstrate this point.

Mercedes, Volvo, and BMW are all luxury cars. Most models have similar features including leather trim, heated seats, driver-assist technology, premium audio systems, and more. Despite the similarities, each has a brand that distinguishes their customers. Volvo brands the word "safety." Buyers who select this car often tout the safety features in addition to luxury. BMW brands the words "driving machine." Their customers are looking for the driving experience of a performance car. Mercedes brands the word "prestige." The car tells others that you have arrived and signals social status.[26]

You can manage the perception others have of you by branding words. I ask a client to pick words (usually no more than three) they want coworkers to use when describing them or their work.

The actual words you wish to brand will depend on the situation. But let's imagine you want to be a chief financial officer of a publicly traded company. What would the best three words be? Think about "ethical," "detail-oriented," and "analytical." "Ethical" would be important to inspire the trust of Wall Street and stock analysts. "Detail-oriented" would signal to all stakeholders that you want to know all the facts and have a deep understanding of the business. "Analytical" would suggest the ability to find and fix problems and seize upon opportunities.

To promote this brand, you would use these words in your resume, speeches, and conversations with others. Using words repeatedly has the same effect as a company advertising its brand on television. But what if you don't like the image coworkers have of you? You can change it through hard work and careful rebranding.

Let's use the example of a wellness officer at an engineering firm. As the wellness officer, you are responsible for promoting the well-being of all employees. Your work is perceived as "touchy-feely" work compared to the engineers'. As such, you soon develop the image of being nice and helpful, but not strategic. In response, you want to be seen as strategic, analytical, and gutsy to better fit into the culture. How do you change people's minds?

The primary tool is to link the word you want in people's minds with your actions. The success formula is:

Use new word + show how your actions represent that image + finish by linking the new word to your actions.

For example, you can expand the image of what a wellness officer does. You might say, "The role of wellness officer is strategic; it focuses on the total well-being of staff including their financial, physical, social, and psychological health. The programs I am introducing are the result of analyzing comprehensive research on the best interventions to promote well-being. Our firm is being gutsy by leading our industry in offering these types of programs and strategic in recognizing their contribution to our success ahead of our competitors. I will always use an analytical and strategic approach to address concerns and capitalize on opportunities."

If the wellness officer continues to link actions to the desired words, it will not take long before their image evolves from "touchy-feely" to "strategic, analytical, and gutsy."

Image and Influence

When leading executive workshops, I include a section on using the Spheres of Influence tool to help participants manage their image and expand their spheres of influence. The ability to influence others is a key skill, and over time you want to expand your breadth of influence (see figure 6.2).

The concept of spheres of influence started as a political term referring to a country or area that has power to affect another without having formal authority. In business, the term evolved to mean a strategy that focuses on attracting customers to you from people you know and people you meet socially, as opposed to pursuing opportunities from strangers.

In development terms, I want clients to nurture their image, based on their knowledge and expertise, to affect others and attract new business based on that image. It is equivalent to the marketing "pull strategy" versus a "push strategy." Rather than pushing to get business and garner resources, you want your image to help pull people toward you and attract resources. It can become a key piece of your personal brand. Evidence that you are a strong leader with a strong brand is that others reach out to you and say they want to work for your company or your department.

Image and your spheres of influence are also important for attracting resources. To illustrate this point, I ask workshop participants to think of money and resources as the physical representation of the collective energy of everyone in the world. The energy flows to those who are the most talented, positive, and passionate. The energy flows to ideas that impact the most people.

A banker sees many great ideas that have no collective energy, therefore no impact. The idea may be ahead of its time, for example. If your goal is growth, I counsel clients never to fall in love with the concept without understanding the collective energy. Let's examine how to expand your spheres of influence throughout your career.

In the beginning of taking on any new role, you want to focus on mastering your craft, which is done through practice, mentoring, and applying your skill across different situations. Malcolm Gladwell talks about the 10,000-hour rule for mastering a skill in his book *Outliers*. In it, he describes the research of psychologist K. Anders Ericsson at the Berlin Academy of Music. Ericsson and his team wanted to determine the factors that differentiated world-class soloists from professional musicians from music teachers in the public school system. Ericsson's study couldn't find any "naturals"—musicians who made it to the top while practicing a fraction of the time their peers did.

"Their research suggests that once a musician has enough ability to get into a top music school, the thing that distinguishes one performer from another is how hard he or she works. That's it. And what's more, the people at the very top don't work just harder or even much harder than everyone else. They work much, much harder."[27]

Figure 6.2. Spheres of Influence

Mastery in a role is the first step to expanding your spheres of influence at the organizational level, and it comes from putting in hours of practice. When I counsel early-in-career professionals, there is an initial tendency to focus on variety and novelty. They work in a job for one year and then want to know what their next job should be. Large organizations have fostered this belief through rotational programs and promoting an "up or out" culture. I encourage young professionals to want nuance as well as novelty. In the long run, you need both a diversity of jobs and diversity of situations in which you have applied your skills. Remember the "T-Shaped" executive? To get to the level of mastery, consider questions like: *Have you done your job during good and bad economic conditions? Can you do your job when you have a supportive, mentoring boss and when you have a demanding but absentee boss?* It takes time and commitment to get to 10,000 hours.

You know when you've begun to master your role because others will ask you to consult. People believe that you are in a position to influence individuals, groups, and organizations with your knowledge, skills, and experience. In the early stages of consulting, you will be asked to mentor and show others who have the same role how to work at higher levels. In later stages of consulting, you'll work across departments and will be seen as a person with the information and/or capability to complete a body of work. You are not responsible to complete the work but are consulted because of your experience. In an emergency situation, you are viewed as someone who can step in and keep a project or initiative on track.

Developing an image as a good consultant is important to your career growth for a few reasons. It:

- Demonstrates that you can influence others without having direct authority—this is an important skill in large, matrixed organizations;
- Signals that you can learn quickly and contribute to the success of others;
- Means you can size up people and situations with an eye to improve a person, process, or idea;
- Highlights valued communication skills, both oral and written;
- Begins to give you an enterprise mindset.

The next rung on the influence ladder within an organization is being viewed as a subject-matter expert (SME). In my work employees often equate this with being a consultant, though there are subtle but important differences. The first is situational. Senior leaders in large companies view SMEs as having more experience and organizational context than consultants. For this reason, SMEs are often put on cross-functional or cross-departmental teams where they are the sole person with a particular body of knowledge. Consultants often work on teams of people with the same expertise.

Senior leaders also give SMEs decision-making authority. They can stand alone and represent the interests of others. Consultants generally analyze current-state situations and make recommendations based on that analysis. SMEs outline strategies, make decisions, and guide initiatives through implementation.

Moe is a typical SME. With more than thirty years of experience in the company, she has done it all in terms of organizational design. She has led teams of people and been an individual contributor. She's worked in the corporate human resources function and worked within business units. She has worked with our executives and frontline managers. She has strong executive presence and a calm disposition. She has reported to me twice in her career. The first time was when I was the VP of Talent Management establishing an organizational consulting unit. The second when I was VP of Talent Development and integrating the Aetna and CVS Health development teams. On both occasions my objective was to remove barriers that got in the way of doing her job. She did not need me but used me as a sounding board for her ideas and work. I looked to Moe to identify where she could add the most value to our department and the organization. That is how we created her annual goals. I trusted her to make decisions, address problems on the fly, and make adjustments as needed. If your boss gives you this type of latitude, then congratulations—you are a subject-matter expert.

At SME level, you are at the top of the organization perception section of the spheres of influence diagram. Most workers are content to stay at this level. And why not? Here, you have mastered your craft, have autonomy in your job, and make considerable positive impact in your company.

But some employees want to climb higher, and to do that they must focus on their industries' perspective of their influence, not just their organization. "Expert" is the first step in expanding your influence from just your organization to an industry. An expert is seen as the authority in an area, just like a subject-matter expert. But the difference at the higher level is that people across the industry trust you as a source of accurate and reliable information on a subject. Image validation as an expert comes from outside your organization, not within it.

In workshops, I cite examples to show when people have successfully expanded their influence in the industry:

- You are quoted in newspaper and magazine articles; they often take the form, "Jane Doe, expert in talent development, says . . ." or "Industry expert Jane Doe believes . . ."
- You are asked to be a member of a panel at an industry conference; you share experience implementing a specific solution or provide views on a topic.
- You write a popular blog or are seen as a social media influencer.
- Authors reference your work in a book or industry white paper.

There are proactive steps you can take to promote your image and expand your influence. If you are the member of an association, offer to speak on a panel or lead a workshop. Conference organizers are always looking for new content. Be proactive and find out about the theme ideas for the next conference. Then write a brief proposal—two or three paragraphs on a workshop you can lead or a panel you can moderate or join. An example of a thirty-second pitch I gave that led to me delivering a workshop on talent development:

In the current issue of *Harvard Business Review*, author Bill Kerr cites executive immersions as a way to get the benefits from talent hot spots without relocating your organization.

For the last six years, CVS Health has designed immersion visits that have accelerated growth for business units, resulted in promotions for participants, and fostered a growth mindset across the organization.

Join me if you would like to learn more and explore.

Another easy way to build your expertise is to read newspapers, magazine articles, and industry trade journals and follow up with the author. Today, writers put their email address or social media contact information at the end of articles. Write the author with a compliment, your credentials, an observation, and a question. An example of a follow-up note to a writer after reading an article on building barriers to affordable housing:

> I enjoyed your recent article in the *Hartford Courant* that outlined barriers middle-class people have finding access to affordable housing [the compliment]; as a mortgage loan officer with more than ten years of experience [your credentials], I believe a lack of understanding of the credit-approval process greatly hinders access to housing [an observation]. Did your investigation uncover a lack of access to credit as a significant contributor [a question]?

Ending the correspondence with a question opens the door for further conversation. Journalists are always looking for reliable sources of information and expertise. Over time, they will reach out to you for quotes.

From expert you evolve to thought leader. A thought leader is more than a pundit you see on television. They are viewed as authoritative (trusted and reliable) and influential. At this point, you are proactively taking steps to influence the image and direction of your entire industry. If you are quoted in the paper or being interviewed on television, you are viewed as a spokesperson for the industry, not just your company.

Looking at crisis is one way to identify and learn from thought leaders. When there is a crisis, where do individuals and the media turn to get information? What actions are they taking so people have faith in the entire industry? Who is asked to predict what is going to happen next and what we should do about it? Thought leaders answer these questions.

The final step in industry influence is to become a visionary. Visionaries think about and plan the future of an industry. They have the imagination, insight, and wisdom to move the industry to the next level. In workshops, I stress that one of the best ways to progress from expert to visionary is to write—articles, books, blogs, etc., and to speak—at conferences, radio and television appearances. Speaking engagements are more personal experiences for people and a way to get across your ideas. But they are limited by your time. Writing and social media are ways to expand the universe of people exposed to your ideas. Writing can be shared with others and translated into many languages. Everyone can discuss, debate, and build upon your ideas.

The final transition is from industry to world. At this level, you have built a track record of success, and your ideas are accepted industry practice. To further expand your influence, you must analyze the factors that resulted in your success and explain them in more generic terms so they can be adapted and adopted outside your industry.

Keen readers will begin to notice a pattern. Breaking things down into a system and using more generic language allows you to cross industries and overcome barriers. The Mapping Your Experience tool helped you break down your resume accomplishment, which was industry specific, into more general transferable skills and milestones. This makes it easier for others outside your industry to understand what you can do. In the leadership chapter, creating a success formula allows others to emulate your ideas for their gain. Describing your ideas in generic terms, with a wider audience, does the same thing with your image and influence.

In the beginning, your ideas and image will impact your local region. As more individuals become aware of you, your image and influence expands throughout your country and then the world.

Oprah Winfrey, billionaire media executive and philanthropist, is an example of how a person expanded her spheres of influence from organization to industry to world leader.

While still attending Tennessee State University, Oprah was a local evening news co-anchor for Nashville's WLAC-TV. Oprah relocated to Chicago and in 1984 hosted a low-rated half-hour morning talk show called *AM Chicago*. She took the show from last place in the ratings to first place, overtaking *Donahue* as the highest-rated talk show in Chicago. At this point, Oprah was at the top of the organizational perception scale, proving that she had the ability to create popular programing.

Oprah jumped to becoming an industry influencer when in 1986 she signed a syndication deal with King World to broadcast her talk show nationally. She renamed the show *The Oprah Winfrey Show*. That program aired for twenty-five seasons, from 1986 to 2011. During that time, Oprah became a visionary and then country and world influencer as the show grew to nearly 212 US stations and more than one hundred countries worldwide. In 2011, Winfrey launched her own TV network, the Oprah Winfrey Network (OWN).

Oprah became a world influencer when her charitable arm, Oprah's Angel Network, raised more than $50 million for charitable programs—she built a leadership academy for girls' education in South Africa and provided relief to the victims of Hurricane Katrina.

In November 2013, Oprah received the nation's highest civilian honor, the Presidential Medal of Freedom, from Barack Obama. The honor both validates and symbolizes Oprah's status as a world influencer.[28]

■ ■ ■

Cultivating your image is important because most of the decisions that impact your career are made when you are not in the room. Consciously crafting your image will promote your personal brand. Use the Spheres of Influence tool to determine your current reach.

When I started Aetna University in 2012, it was difficult to get younger talent into the human resources department. After speaking with a number of colleagues, it was clear that managers thought new college graduates did not have the maturity or skills necessary for our entry-level jobs. What was needed was a radical change in image.

Working with team member Christine Valluzzi, who has a passion for developing talent, we created the HR Leadership Development Program (HRLDP). I worked to recruit the first class of three graduates from the top undergraduate universities. Christine expanded our summer internship program to serve as a pipeline for future classes. Two people we recruited were from Cornell University, which has a premier human resources program. Shay Familoni and Stephanie Selvius joined the initial class. I got to know them when serving as a guest lecturer for Professor Lisa Dragoni's Designing Learning Solutions in Organizations course. The third recruit was Jennifer Paxton, an honors graduate with a dual degree from the University of North Carolina and Duke University (for the record, she considers herself a Tar Heel, not a Blue Devil).

Managers were skeptical but supportive of the new colleagues. Jennifer worked in our organizational consulting department and helped design support materials for HR generalists. She also worked on Aetna's acquisition of Coventry Health Care. Jennifer's boss, Phil Lohr, was not sure a young professional had the gravitas to lead parts of a complex acquisition. But after three months, Phil stopped by my office and said, "I was wrong, Jennifer is doing an outstanding job and I would take another HRLDP in a heartbeat." Jennifer changed the image people had of early-in-career talent.

Stephanie became an HR business consultant, an important role involving counseling business leaders on a variety of subjects including talent acquisition, performance management, organizational design, and employee-relations issues. Stephanie's calm professional demeanor and reputation for producing actionable analytical insights changed the image of early-in-career talent from being unable to work with high-level business leaders to one of valuable partner.

Shay served a dual role, working as a talent management consultant and compensation analyst. She presented her findings to teams of leaders and served as a spokesperson and cheerleader for the new program. Shay changed the image HR leaders had from not being able to handle the complexity of one role to performing two jobs while helping to recruit the next class of associates.

Shay went on to get a law degree and master's in business administration from the University of Pennsylvania. She works as an attorney in Washington, DC. Jennifer got her MBA from Michigan and is a brand manager at Johnson & Johnson. We are lucky to still have Stephanie with the organization, where she is an HR business partner.

Fast-forward to today and Christine leads a program where CVS Health leaders fight to get the chance for HRLDP associates to work in their department, and managers line up to hire recent program graduates.

Bottom line: Performance is important, especially early in your career, but image and your spheres of influence count more as you climb the corporate ladder.

Image is crucial. For most of us it involves communicating our direct experience in a way that causes others to have a positive perception of us. This allows us to get the jobs, promotions, and assignments we desire. But what if you like your job and are not angling to get a promotion right now? That doesn't mean you should neglect development. The majority of development occurs in your current role, and that is the subject of the next chapter.

CHAPTER 7

Development Plan:
Create Your Success Blueprint

If you are planning for a year, grow rice; if you are
planning for a decade, grow trees; if you are planning
for a lifetime, grow people.

Chinese proverb

The clients that come to me for help generally fall into one of two
groups. The first group is happy in their current role, want to stay,
but don't want to stagnate. They hope to gain new skills and knowledge,
so they can continue to grow and develop. The second group wants a
new job or assignment within their company or outside their current
organization or industry.

A lot of the tips and tools in this book have been devoted to the second group because the task is often more difficult. That said, it is true
that most employees will stay in their current role and develop in place.
It is also true that it takes time, energy, and planning to continuously
grow and develop in your current role. Failure to invest in yourself can
lead to outdated skills, stale knowledge, and fewer opportunities for
interesting assignments.

Job requirements are not stagnant; they evolve and generally
require higher levels of skill, judgment, and interaction with technology over time. Just think about the simple task of depositing or

cashing a check. I spent a summer as a bank teller, mostly working at the drive-up window. Every Thursday and Friday people stood in line in the branch waiting to deposit and cash their checks at lunchtime. I'd see a snaking line of cars waiting to be served at my window. Our branch was open 10 AM to 4 PM. We closed at 2 PM on Wednesdays and were open on Saturday from 9 AM to noon. Not very convenient hours for customers. After college I still had to deposit my check, but there were these new automated teller machines that allowed me to skip the teller and deposit the check. Soon after that, my employer electronically deposited my pay directly into my checking account so now I only went to the ATM when I wanted cash. Fast-forward to today, and I can take a picture of a check with my phone and it is automatically deposited into my account. I use my debit card to pay for purchases instead of cash.

Scientists and strategists distinguish trends into two groups: slow and fast change. Some changes occur rapidly, within seconds or minutes. An earthquake, a fire, or ice melting in the hot sun are examples. When change is fast and/or dramatic, we tend to notice the effects, react to the change, and want to prepare in case it happens again. We design buildings that can withstand ground shifts, use less flammable construction materials, install smoke alarms and sprinkler systems, and put ice in insulated cups.

Other changes occur slowly, over days, months, and years. The banking changes happened over the past thirty years, but their impact was significant. A tree growing is another example of a slow change. I want you to think of your current job as a slow-change event. Changes to your responsibilities gradually but continuously occur and make dramatic shifts when viewed over a period of years. Going back to our teller example, in the beginning it was a transactional job. You were rewarded for processing banking transactions rapidly and accurately. Picture four tellers behind a counter. One person was the "head teller" who had the most money and experience and helped the rest of the tellers if they had a problem. Two tellers processed general transactions and handled most of the customers. The fourth teller focused on business owners and their large deposits. If there were no business owners in line, they helped with the general overflow. If two business owners came in at the same time, one had to wait for the other to finish.

With the rise of ATMs and direct deposit usage, the need for tellers dropped. Which tellers got to stay and which were laid off? Tellers who knew how to process transactions accurately, understood business clients, and were willing to learn how to interact with new technology were retained. Go into a branch today, and the person behind the counter who used to be a "teller" is now a "client services representative" who knows how to deposit your check, sell you investment products, and service your loans.

The purpose of this chapter is to understand four components of developing in a role (see figure 7.1). Then use that understanding to create a simple plan that serves as a blueprint for continued success. I call it the Development Plan tool (see worksheet 6). Research varies on how much of a person's development can be attributed to a specific component, so unlike the Networking Quadrant tool, I have not included percentages. Most agree that work experiences account for the majority of development. I recommend spending equal time in the other three areas.

Figure 7.1. Developing in Your Role

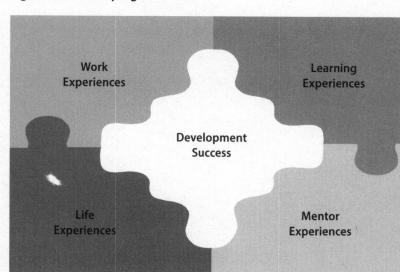

Work Experiences

Learning Experiences

Development Success

Life Experiences

Mentor Experiences

Worksheet 6: Development Plan

Work Experiences	Describe two new job experiences you will have over the next twelve months.

1.

2.

Learning Experiences	Identify two learning experiences you will have over the next twelve months.

•

•

Mentor Experiences	Identify two mentors.

• Work Experience Mentor:

• Learning Experience Mentor:

Life Experiences	Identify two outside work experiences that will help you in your current role.

•

•

Worksheet 6: Development Plan (continued)

Succession Plans	Key Question
List three roles or people you could replace if you changed jobs: 1. Role/Current Person in the Role 2. Role/Current Person in the Role 3. Role/Current Person in the Role	"What is one thing that, if improved, would make me succeed at a higher level within the organization?"

Work Experiences

Practical work experiences represent the biggest opportunity to develop in a role. Other people have written extensively on this subject, but I want to highlight two concepts that I've found the most useful in my client work. The first concept comes from Mark Kizilos, author of the book *FrameBreaking Leadership Development* (see figure 7.2). It is the concept of intensity and stretch as the key drivers of on-the-job development. To help people grow on the job, we need to determine which experiences an employee needs to be successful in the organization and what they should learn from those experiences.

On the vertical axis is intensity. *Intensity* is the extent to which an experience involves higher performance demands than an individual has faced in prior career experiences. According to Kizilos, one must *thrive* to survive in such situations. Examples of intensity might be time pressure—you have less time than usual to complete a task. Or you are assigned a project that has greater visibility to senior management.[29]

On the horizontal axis is stretch. *Stretch* describes the extent to which an experience pushes one outside an area of expertise, background, or preparation. A person must *reach* to master the new situation. Examples of stretch might be assignments that require you to build relationships with new people outside your area of expertise or learning a new skill to accomplish a task.[30]

Figure 7.2. Mark Kizilos's FrameBreaking Model

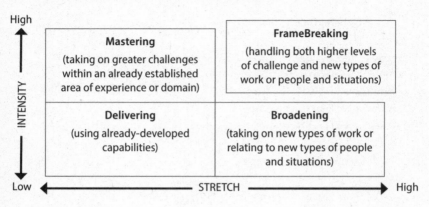

Using Kizilos's model, you can categorize your job experiences into one of four buckets:

1. **Delivering Experience:** familiar work, situations, and people under normal time lines
2. **Broadening Experience:** new work, situations, and/or people under normal time lines
3. **Mastering Experience:** familiar work but higher-stakes situations and intense time lines
4. **FrameBreaking Experience:** new work, situations, and/or people under intense time lines

The second concept comes from Cynthia McCauley from the Center for Creative Leadership, who identified ten key leadership challenges you must learn how to manage during your career.[31]

1. **Unfamiliar Responsibilities:** handling new or very different responsibilities
2. **New Directions:** starting something new or making strategic changes
3. **Inherited Problems:** fixing problems created by someone else
4. **Problems with Employees:** dealing with incompetent, inexperienced, or change-resistant employees

5. **High Stakes:** managing tight deadlines, pressure from above, and high-visibility responsibilities
6. **Scope and Scale:** handling work broad in scope or large in sheer size
7. **External Pressure:** managing interface with important groups outside the organization (e.g., customers)
8. **Influencing Without Authority:** influencing peers, higher management, or other key people
9. **Work Across Cultures:** working with people from different cultures, institutions, or countries
10. **Work Group Diversity**: working with people of both genders and different ethnic/racial backgrounds

Combining these two concepts, we can fill out the Work Experiences section of the Development Plan (refer to worksheet 6) taking the following steps:

1. Pick one or two areas of development; if you are stuck, refer to Cynthia McCauley's list.
2. Imagine it is twelve months from now and you have been successful in your role; write a resume accomplishment for your job experience using the STAR Method described in chapter 3.
3. Share, validate, and edit your resume accomplishment with your manager.
4. Get your manager's input to categorize your job assignment into one of the four buckets (Delivering, Broadening, Mastering, or FrameBreaking).
5. Identify the skills you will practice achieving your resume accomplishment.
6. Get feedback from others on your progress.
7. Validate with your manager that you have achieved your resume accomplishment.

Now you can describe the two new job experiences you will have over the next twelve months. Below are some examples:

- Consult with a team that has fallen behind schedule implementing a new software release (broadening experience working with an inherited problem); provide consulting skills and establish new governance and work processes that result in the successful 2.0 software release on time and on budget.
- Manage new-hire training for one hundred new sales associates versus fifty last year (delivering experience working on a larger scale); design and deliver new hire-training for the Northeast and Midwest sales offices, achieve a net promoter score of 85 percent.
- Accept promotion from head of government relations for the state of California to head of government affairs for our federal office in Washington, DC (mastering experience with external pressures); successfully implement our lobbying agenda and shape the content of new environmental regulation.
- Move from head of Medicare in West region to retail divisional vice president (FrameBreaking experience with unfamiliar responsibilities); grow the retail business by 15 percent by introducing more profitable products and services targeted to seniors.

Learning Experiences

Learning experiences, both formal and informal, are important. Continually working to improve our strengths while adding new skills is key to career success. So why is it so difficult to read that relevant article, practice that new skill, or try a different approach? Are you having flashbacks to school, sitting in a classroom, bored and wishing you were outside playing while the teacher talks and writes on a whiteboard?

I have good news and better news. First, the good news. It's okay, and some believe natural, to dislike learning, studying, and training, but like eating your vegetables, it is good for you. So why the natural dislike for learning? Learning and training forces you to do two things we don't like—think and act. But there is no learning without acting, and in the case of learning that means doing something that is often unfamiliar to us. And there is no learning without reflecting, thinking about why something worked or did not work. Research supports our natural reluctance for thinking and acting.

People hate sitting and thinking so much that they will literally shock themselves to avoid it. Psychology professors Dan Gilbert of Harvard and Tim Wilson of the University of Virginia asked undergraduates to sit in a room with a color picture of a cockroach while classical guitar music played in the background. Also in the room was a button that produced a mild electric shock. Students were given five dollars and asked if they would pay money to avoid the shock. Seventy-six percent said they would pay. But when placed in the room and asked just to think, the majority of people started shocking themselves voluntarily. One person shocked themself 190 times in fifteen minutes![32]

We also favor inaction to action, what Daniel Kahneman and Amos Tversky labeled "The Action-Effect." People tend to feel greater regret over negative outcomes if they are a result of action compared to inaction. In their studies two investors invested in Company A. One investor switched their investment from Company A to Company B, while the other took no action. Both lost the same amount of money, but people attributed higher regret to the investor that acted and switched.[33]

My job is to develop the next generation of leaders despite these two pitfalls. Luckily, I have two things going for me: time and community. Time weakens and even reverses the Action Effect as we view the training in broader, more abstract terms. Time changes the way we perceive and think of our actions. I can get you to think differently and change behavior when you see the changes as normal, justified, and accepted by your social circle. Workshop participants want to fit in, not stick out. That is why we like to have in-person cohorts in training, so participants can support each other and change together.

That was the good news—your feelings are normal. Now the better news. We know a lot more about how adults learn that can help accelerate development. The keys to engaged learning are:

- Know the *why* before we share the *what*—why is this learning experience important and how will it help me do a better job?

- When you introduce a new idea, process, etc., connect it to how you should act on the job—no abstract, philosophical thinking; focus on the practical.
- Offer variety and choice—individuals learn in different ways, so provide options for the visual, auditory, and kinesthetic learners, the extroverts and the introverts.
- Reinforce learning through appreciation, feedback, and evaluation—if learners don't see the results of trying something new, they will stop doing it.

Armed with this information, you are now ready to fill out the Learning Experiences section of the Development Plan. I prefer that clients focus on one or two major learning topics in a year. Imagine you wanted to develop consulting skills.

Christine manages our Human Resources Leadership Development Program, a three-year rotational program designed to prepare new graduates for future HR leadership roles. One of the key skills HR professionals need is consulting, so that is part of their development plan. Christine uses all the engaged learning keys to build and reinforce this skill.

Begin with the Why. Christine starts with *why*—developing expertise in consulting is foundational to be a successful HR leader. Consulting skills are needed to develop talent, handle employee relations issues, manage colleagues, lead projects, and handle contract negotiations, just to name a few.

Make the Connection. Program associates are given guides and tool kits for what good consulting looks like and sounds like. Colleagues share their experiences and lessons learned from consulting with business leaders.

Offer Variety and Choice. Associates read the book *Flawless Consulting* by Peter Block, which serves as a reference manual. Christine assigns associates different rotations, forcing them to use consulting skills in different situations under different conditions. Associates meet and role-play different scenarios to practice consulting skills and get feedback.

Reinforce. Christine meets one-on-one with associates to provide coaching and evaluation. She shares appreciation from rotational managers and asks senior associates to teach new associates and summer interns, further ingraining the knowledge.

Go back to worksheet 6 and write two learning experiences. Work with your manager and/or others to identify *why* it is important and *how* you will develop the skill over the next year. Set up quarterly check-in points to evaluate your progress. Finally, take the time to reflect on what worked best so you can repeat that success, as well as change what you need to be even more effective in the future.

Mentor Experiences

We all need mentors. Mentors advise, guide, and offer support so mentees can achieve their career goals. In their book *Peak: Secrets from the New Science of Expertise*, Anders Ericsson and Robert Pool describe three levels of practice. *Naïve practice* is just the generic repetition of actions where you get no feedback or coaching. You may get better and develop skills, but it will likely be slower and based on luck.[34]

Purposeful practice is focused, where students are required to give it their full attention. They get feedback that is immediate and specific on where they are falling short. It requires students to leave their comfort zones, pushing them beyond what is comfortable and familiar.[35]

Deliberate practice pushes people out of their comfort zones and involves feedback and focus but is based on proven techniques developed by past experts. The student is going down a predictable path of success.[36]

Ideally you want one mentor to help you achieve the work experience goals of your development plan, while another mentor will assist with your learning experiences. Go back to worksheet 6 and write two names.

Life Experiences

Experiences outside of work are a great source of development that are often ignored or underappreciated. There are many advantages to using nonwork experiences to grow and develop. Life experiences:

- Offer a safer environment to practice new skills outside the eyes of your boss and peers;
- Provide opportunities to take on greater decision-making authority and leadership responsibilities;
- Expand your network and spheres of influence outside your company and/or industry;
- Teach you how to influence without direct authority and build coalitions to get things done;
- Allow you to control the time you invest and select an experience that has a distinct beginning, middle, and end.

I advise clients to volunteer for a not-for-profit organization. It helps your community while you hone your skills. Look for something you have a natural interest in or passion for. Imagine you have a basket in your hand, while the not-for-profit organization has a basket in their hand. You put money, your strengths, and experiences into their basket. In exchange, you would like the organization to put different responsibilities, opportunities, and connections into your basket.

A few years ago, I joined the board of Achieve Hartford, a local not-for-profit organization activating private sector leaders to solve education problems. By doing so we hope to close the achievement gap between Hartford students and their suburban neighbors. When I first joined, I offered financial, strategic, and human resources expertise, and some knowledge of education. The board offered me the opportunity to build a Connecticut network and greater understanding of the educational system. Although I had served on previous boards, those were in Massachusetts. After twenty years in the Boston area, I was starting over in a new state. Participating on the board gave me immediate access to local leaders. I also got to learn new skills by working as a member of the development committee. I had never been in charge of a capital campaign, nor did I know a lot about general fundraising, grants, and foundations. The board provided a safe environment to learn and try out new skills with experienced staff and other board members.

Board service is one of many ways to use life experiences. Consider:

- Working a part-time job: I ask entrepreneurs and industry shifters to do this before making a major investment or life change.
- Coaching a sports team: this helps build leadership skills.
- Writing a blog, magazine, or newspaper article: this builds communication skills and tests your ideas with a wider audience.
- Traveling to another country or offering to be the guide for an expatriate worker: this provides an understanding of other cultures.
- Working on a political campaign or for a special interest group: this will teach you how to manage tight timelines under stress.
- Providing consulting services to smaller organizations outside your industry: this offers the opportunity to practice your skills in a new environment.
- Mentoring students: tutoring expands your network and develops leadership skills.
- Learning something totally new like riding horses, painting, mountain climbing, or sailing: stretching yourself gets you in touch with the beginner's mindset.
- Taking a course in a subject you know nothing about: this opens your brain to new experiences.
- Asking a much younger person to teach you a new skill (reverse mentoring): this develops empathy and respect for people from different generations.

Now go back to worksheet 6 and identify two outside-of-work experiences that will help you in your current role.

Succession Plans

In this part of the development plan, list three roles you would consider taking and the people you could replace if you changed jobs. Even if you like your job, you need to expand your skills and network because that job will evolve over time—remember the teller example? Whether through technology, process improvement, or management expectations, major responsibilities across different jobs tend to aggregate over months and years. By identifying the roles and the workers in those roles, it gives you a road map for what skills and experiences you have to add to absorb additional responsibilities.

Fill in the roles and employees in worksheet 6. Set up networking meetings with those coworkers. Ask them how their jobs have changed over time and what experiences, skills, and education someone would need in the future to be successful in their role.

Key Question

The final part of the development plan is the key question. You can't answer this question yourself. You need the input from your boss and/or other leaders senior to you. The goal is to identify the one thing that, if improved, would make you a success at a higher level in the organization.

By focusing on one thing, instead of two, three, or five, you force the person to identify what is most important. Many clients, whether being proactive, or because they feel their boss is too busy to consult, create their development plan in a vacuum. The quality of the plan is only as good as the quality of the inputs. The key question helps you to seek better input. The question also links improvement to success. I see many plans that say "improve communication skills," for example. But will better communication skills lead to higher levels of success? If yes, great; if not, then it should not be a focus of the development plan.

Make It a Living Document

You've spent the time creating a robust but focused development plan. Make it a living document by reviewing it periodically and getting input from others. As needed, update it to reflect the new reality of your work and circumstance.

Two Plus One Theory

Using the Development Plan tool takes time and energy, so why do it? Over the years I've observed and worked with many successful leaders across business, government, and philanthropy. Many of them develop a towering strength over time. But I've noticed that highly successful leaders develop two strengths, one of which is unusual for their field. This, coupled with emotional intelligence, propels their success. Hence the term Two Plus One Theory. The ultimate goal of your development plan is to develop two towering strengths, one of which is unique to your industry or role, and add emotional intelligence to get to three. Success often comes from bringing a different perspective or mindset to a problem, area, or field.

Step 1: Identify and Develop Your Core Strength

For any given field or endeavor there is a core strength or mindset that will enable you to be successful. The owner of a dance studio would have physical intelligence at their core. If you are going to be a screenwriter, then building linguistic intelligence is important. The first step is to identify and build the core intelligence that will enable you to become technically competent in your field. Refer to your towering strength, which we discussed in chapter six.

Step 2: Develop a Unique Secondary Strength

Identifying, developing, and using the right core intelligence for your job will give you the foundation for success. Developing a secondary strength, which allows you to bring a new perspective to your business or industry, can be a source of differentiation and creativity. Creative people often combine at least two strengths or mindsets, one of which is unusual for that business or industry.

According to research conducted by neuropsychologist Sandra Witelson and described in the article "The Exceptional Brain of Albert Einstein," Einstein had outstanding logical-mathematical intelligence like most physicists, but his spatial capacities were extraordinary for a physicist, which allowed him to bring a diverse perspective and creative insight.[37]

Case Study: Authentic Entertainment

Tom Rogan, cofounder and president of Authentic Entertainment, a California-based television production company, is an example of successfully developing a core and secondary strength and mindset.

When you relax in front of your television, there is a good chance the network you're watching did not produce your favorite television show. The sitcom, movie, drama, or reality show was conceived, produced, and sold to the network by an independent production company. At its core, television involves the ability to create and manipulate visual patterns and images to tell a compelling story. Tom consciously and unconsciously developed this strength, allowing him to be successful in his field. Tom's parents are friends of my family, so I got to see Tom grow up.

As a child, Tom's hobbies, interests, and play activities unconsciously developed spatial and visual intelligence. He borrowed camcorders and made short films with friends. He developed his creative skills making short comedies parodying teenage suburban life. Working for the National Audubon Society, Tom developed an appreciation for the environment and natural world. Even his hobbies, like playing chess, revolve around recognizing and visualizing patterns. A good chess player can envision what the board will look like in five to ten moves. Tom's choices built his spatial abilities at a time when most boys his age focus on physical intelligence (organized sports, crafts like woodworking, or a trade).

Tom consciously developed spatial and visual abilities by majoring in television and mass communication at Emerson College. While there he honed the technical skills involved with production—lighting, camera angles, set design, props, directing, hiring of actors, etc. His shows won a number of awards and aired on a local Boston independent station. Tom's background and foundation in spatial intelligence allowed him to garner positions of increasing responsibility with production companies after graduation. But Tom's possession of a secondary strength and intelligence—logical/mathematical—differentiated him from others in his field and increased his ability to be a successful entrepreneur.

One of the common jobs on the ladder to becoming an executive producer is to be a production manager. Tom held this position with two companies prior to starting his own company. The production manager is responsible for developing and managing the budget and overseeing all aspects of a show's production. An ideal competency or skill for someone to manage this process would be a high level of logical/math intelligence—someone who is good with numbers and has the capacity to analyze and solve problems logically. People with strength in this type of intelligence are not usually associated with, or attracted to, production. A more typical intelligence combination found in media and entertainment is spatial/linguistic, like Shonda Rhimes, the creator of such shows as *Grey's Anatomy, Scandal, How to Get Away with Murder,* and *The Catch.* Another combination is physical/spatial. Ron Howard or Penny Marshall come to mind with this mix, as they successfully made the transition from actors to director/producers.

Tom cofounded Authentic Entertainment in 2000 with Lauren Lexton. Tom brought the unusual combination of spatial/logical/math knowledge to television production. In Tom's words, "I would go into companies and see things were inefficient. It was obvious to me what was wrong. I'd strip away everything that was not important and create a system to organize the work."

But it was not obvious to everyone else. Not possessing his type of intelligence, people assumed chaos and frenetic production sets were the industry norm. Over time, Tom and Lauren developed an integrated system of databases to track how money was spent on a production. This system allowed the producer to make better, more informed, creative decisions because they knew how much, where, and why money was spent. Tom's logical/math intelligence allowed him to differentiate himself from other production managers and producers. He developed a reputation for delivering high-quality programming on budget and on time. Other production companies have used his software and systems for managing their projects.

Tom's unique combination for his industry helped Authentic Entertainment become a success. He and Lauren oversaw the creation and production of hit shows such as *Ace of Cakes*, *Knife Fight*, *Here Comes Honey Boo Boo*, *Flipping Out!*, *Best Thing I Ever Ate*, and *Toddlers & Tiaras*. After building the business over a number of years, Tom and Lauren sold the company to Endemol Shine in 2010.

Tom retired from the production business, moved back East, and has recently started a new company with his wife, Monica. Their company, Goodnow Farms Chocolate, sources cacao beans directly from farmers throughout Latin America and uses them to craft fine-flavor, single-origin chocolate.

Case Study Insights

- Identify expertise, knowledge, and skills that are uncommon for a given role or industry. This can serve as your source of competitive advantage. Tom's example showed how common business financial and budgeting skills positively impacted television production. Design thinking, a common practice used in the arts and architecture, is currently transforming the way business thinks about creating new products to meet customer needs.
- Look to your past to see what naturally attracts you. I often tell clients that what you are good at is what you've done your whole life. In Tom's case, he has been making up stories and using a camera since he was a child. Over time, he honed his craft through job experiences, formal education, and being mentored by others. What have you done and enjoyed doing your whole life?

Emotional Intelligence Is the Plus One

Emotional intelligence turbocharges your strengths. Daniel Goleman's *Emotional Intelligence: Why It Can Matter More Than IQ* defines emotional intelligence as the capacity to recognize our own feelings and those of others, the ability to motivate ourselves, and to manage emotions effectively in ourselves and others.[38] EQ includes the following four characteristics:

- **Self-Awareness**—the ability to recognize one's emotions and their effects, knowing your strengths and limits, and having a strong sense of your self-worth and capabilities
- **Self-Management**—the ability to keep disruptive emotions and impulses in check, maintaining standards of honesty and integrity, taking responsibility for personal performance, adapting to change, and striving to improve and act on opportunities
- **Social Awareness**—the ability to sense others' feelings and take an active interest in their concerns, recognizing a group's emotional state and power relationships, and anticipating and meeting customers' needs
- **Social Skills**—the ability to sense other's developmental needs and support their development, inspiring and guiding groups and individuals, persuading others, listening effectively, initiating and managing change, negotiating and resolving disagreements, nurturing key relationships, and working with others toward a common goal

Emotional intelligence provides a strong foundation that supports the other strengths. The ability to understand others and taking an active interest in their concerns is a cornerstone to innovation. Individuals and organizations that are not innovative often suffer from an "I" perspective that prevents them from seeing the world from the lens of their customers. As a result, innovation is based upon internal capabilities instead of external customer needs and experiences.

The ability to sense others' needs and feelings and support their development will enable you to attract and motivate teams of people. Emotional intelligence gives individuals the skills to nurture relationships and guide teams of workers to focus on achieving a specific goal.

Finally, emotional intelligence is key to forming partnerships and developing alliances. Successful partnerships and joint ventures are a result of mutual respect, understanding, cooperation, and trust. All of these attributes take time to develop, but emotional intelligence skills like active listening, negotiation, and conflict resolution can accelerate the process.

■ ■ ■

Your current job is the best source of experience and knowledge growth. Use the Development Plan tool to systematically accelerate your career by adding learning, mentoring, and life experiences.

Eric felt stuck. He had been a benefit consultant for the past six years. He was ambitious, a hard worker, and a good leader. I met Eric when he became part of my mentoring circle. The goal was to partner senior leaders with five to six midlevel leaders. We met once a month to discuss work challenges and opportunities, and answer any questions. Group sessions were followed up with individual meetings to work on tailored development plans.

Eric was frustrated because his plan was not producing the results he wanted. Learning? Eric had that covered: he went back to school to get a master of science in communication. In addition, he got a certification in project management to separate himself from his peers. Life experiences: check. Eric served as program director for the Connecticut Basketball Club, managing sixteen youth basketball teams that traveled across the country. This gave Eric advanced leadership experience, exposure across the country, and a positive image as an organization-centered leader. Work? Eric was a high performer with good ratings. He had done all he could do by himself. What he needed was a sponsor.

I served in that role, contacting managers I knew and highlighting Eric's potential. Eric had many of the elements of the development plan. He just needed someone to help connect him to future opportunities. In a short period of time, Eric became a sales associate in our middle market group. He continued to increase his spheres of influence by serving as chair of the African American Employee Resource Group. He received another promotion and eventually was recruited by a competitor to take on a larger role.

Eric's success stems from his dedication to learning both inside and outside his day-to-day job.

Bottom line: The world is your classroom, take advantage of all it has to offer.

Developing in place covers the majority of employees. Armed with the Development Plan tool and the Two Plus One Theory, you have the tools to continually develop in your role. But what if we don't have a lot of direct experience or we want to shift the direction of our careers? And what about the additional barriers that some professionals face? Well, those are the topics I'll cover in the next part of the book.

PART II

Special Circumstances

CHAPTER 8

Making Transitions:
Moving from One Industry to Another

Life is pleasant. Death is peaceful. It's the transition
that's troublesome.

—*Isaac Asimov*

Whenever I give a development talk or workshop, the most frequently asked question I get is: "How did you change jobs and/
or careers?"

The question initially surprised me, and, in my thirties, I would give
the funny but painfully true answer: "It only took twenty-one interviews
and thank-you notes to move from teaching to banking." But the question
kept coming in voices that expressed frustration, anger, hurt, and hope-
lessness. So I decided to give the topic more thought.

I've been lucky to make transitions across industries and roles. As
I mentioned, I started out in education, transitioned to banking, then
healthcare, then consulting, and finally back to healthcare. My roles
have included teaching, commercial lending, chief of staff, mergers and
acquisitions, strategy, and consulting and human resources. Reflecting
on my transitions, I attribute my success to two factors. First, I adopted
a mindset of equating a transition with learning a foreign language.
Second, I used a systematic consultative advisory sales approach to get
the new job.

Adopt the Mindset of Learning a Foreign Language

If you've tried to learn a foreign language, you know how difficult it can be. Traditional methods include memorizing vocabulary, learning to conjugate verbs, and reciting numbers, days of the week, and common phrases in halting speech. In elementary and high school, this is how I attempted to learn French, Latin, and Spanish. But I had an entirely different experience in college.

I studied Spanish using the Rassias Method, also known as the Dartmouth Intensive Language Model, in college. Professor Rassias used a theatrical, immersive approach to teaching foreign languages to students. I spent four days per week studying Spanish. Over a ten-week period I was exposed to a three-prong approach to learning a new language that resulted in students becoming proficient in speaking a foreign language. A traditional classroom with a professor was the first component, but he or she never spoke English! They used gestures, pointed at objects in the room, and applauded when we got the right answer.

Drill instructors were the second component. These were usually junior professors or language majors. Because I worked and played on the freshman tennis team, I had to attend the early morning drill sessions. Making an eighteen-year-old get up at 8 AM to practice a foreign language is not usually a recipe for success. But the classes were exciting. The instructors were animated, used visual aids, and demanded that everyone participate. Charles Stansfield and Jeanne Hornor described the approach in their paper, "The Dartmouth/Rassias Model for Teaching Foreign Languages":

> Small groups of five to eight students meet five hours per week with apprentice teachers, who are responsible for reinforcing what has been taught in the master session. Here the teacher strives for a high rate of response through the use of rapid-fire drills . . . an average of sixty-five responses per student per one-hour session should be obtained. Rassias' technique for conducting drills includes four parts as follows: a) teacher models or gives a cue; b) teacher snaps their fingers; c) teacher points to a student; and d) teacher employs intense eye contact.[39]

Language lab was the final component. Students sit at a desk with headphones listening to native speakers review grammar and describe everyday experiences they would face if traveling to another country. For example, one lab may describe a person calling for a taxi, going to a local market to buy food, and reading a recipe to prepare dinner. Labs are a way to listen to native speakers and get comfortable with the rhythm, pace, and nuances of a language.

The Dartmouth/Rassias Model continues to be popular and successful, with more than 50 percent of undergraduates studying abroad in one of Dartmouth's own distinctive programs, which are led by faculty members.[40]

Getting a job in a new or different industry, company, or role requires a mindset shift like the one required to learn a foreign language. The three parts of the Dartmouth/Rassias Model can be used as a guide to find a new job:

1. formal learning and guidance from an expert in the target job (the professor);
2. practice speaking the new language (the drill instructors); and
3. listening to workers who have the job you want speaking with each other in common work situations (language lab).

Guidance from an expert in the field is the first step. You need to network with people who can help you understand the employer or hiring manager perspective (see chapter 2). They will help you identify the experiences, knowledge, skills, and education you need to qualify for the role. With this information, you can begin to build the bridge between your experience and the new job. Taking courses and reading books and industry trade magazines are examples of formal learning.

You must become comfortable speaking the language of the new industry. The drill instructors forced you to speak up, voice your opinions, and fail in a safe environment. In the beginning your speech will be halted and slow as you "think" about what you want to say, but after enough practice and support something magical happens: you stop "translating" in your mind and just begin to think and speak in the new language. In college everyone remembers when they had their first dream in a foreign language. When you begin to dream in the language of the new industry, you know you are on your way to competence. Get together with someone who has worked in your target industry for years. Your job is to speak on any topic for twenty to thirty minutes. They force you to answer questions, share opinions, and make predictions about the future of the industry. Their role is only to correct factual errors and encourage you to keep talking. This practice will prepare you for interviews. You will be comfortable expressing your opinions during those interviews. In contrast, most job candidates will appear nervous and sound unnatural as they recite memorized answers to questions. How you carry yourself and the flow of your conversation is much more important than the truth of your arguments.

Finding a "language lab" for your new industry or role is the final piece of the puzzle. You need to see experts in action talking about your target industry. Luckily, the internet makes this much easier today. In the old days, I would go to industry conferences, chamber dinners, and lectures to hear experts talk about their field. If you were lucky, experts were interviewed on a major television network. Today, the internet easily connects you to YouTube videos, podcasts, blogs, TED Talks, and other sources. Your job is to listen for common approaches or "schools of thought." After a while you will recognize the patterns in strategy (what they focus on and why it is important), business model (how they deliver value to customers), and structure (how they organize to get work done).

Now that you are comfortable speaking the language of the new industry or role, it's time to make the transition and get the job. The best way I know is to use a consultative advisory sales approach.

Consultative Advisory Sales Approach

The consultative approach has three parts:

1. establishing the relationship with the hiring manager;
2. qualifying the opportunity; and
3. closing the deal.

It is important to remember that your goal is to solve a specific problem for the hiring manager. If the manager is looking for general talent and not trying to solve a specific problem, then you will not be hired. I guesstimate that 80 percent of open positions will be filled by people who have direct experience doing the job. You are looking for the 20 percent of opportunities where the manager is frustrated with his or her inability to solve a specific problem. Alternatively, they could be upgrading staff to prepare for a new or different future. This is the environment necessary for them to take a chance on someone from another industry or with an unusual background.

Establishing the Relationship

First, you must know yourself to forge the relationship. You can't get *where* you want if you don't know *what* you want. Identify your skills, talents, and interests, and be able to make the connection to the new opportunity. You know when you have a skill because you can tell three ninety-second stories that highlight your use of that skill. The stories should follow the traditional STAR Method of Situation or Task given, the Actions you took, and the Results (refer to chapter 3 where I go into greater detail about the method). Also, know why you want to work in the new industry or role. What attracts you? What difference can you make or value can you add? Armed with this information, you are ready to establish relationships by bonding and building rapport with hiring managers.

Managers looking for talent tend to hire applicants they know and trust. This is even more important when they decide to take a chance on someone with less direct experience. Their decision will be more emotional than logical. If they were relying on logic, they would select a candidate with more experience and a track record of success in the same role. You want them to feel comfortable and say, "Trust me, we need you to solve this problem." That means establishing a bond with the hiring manager like an old friend or colleague. Artfully look for connections and links. Did you and the hiring manager:

- grow up in the same part of the country, state, or town?
- attend the same schools, or are your schools in the same conference or district?

- share the same religious traditions, values, etc.?
- have the same type of early-in-career training (e.g., financial analysis, retail experience, or military service)?

Also look to the present, to see if the hiring manager and you:

- share the same hobbies or leisure activities?
- have the same number of kids or live in the same part of the country, state, or town?
- like the same professional or college sports teams?
- like the same music, authors, etc.?

These are not trivial questions; your goal is to find connections that counter your lack of industry experience and job history. After making the hiring manager comfortable, you are now ready to determine if you will be seriously considered for this opportunity or if the hiring manager is just being polite. The key is to find one or two points to start a more natural conversation. Remember, as I mentioned in chapter 2, you are not an investigative reporter or cyber stalker! You are not trying to impress interviewers with your research skills, you are just looking for areas of similar interest or connection.

Qualifying the Opportunity

Research shows that people make decisions emotionally. In his book, *Management Rewired: Why Feedback Doesn't Work and Other Surprising Lessons from the Latest Brain Science,* Charles Jacobs highlights the work of neurologist Antonio Damasio:[41]

> But according to the neurologist Antonio Damasio, the seat of our conscious thought, the prefrontal cortex, has a reciprocal connection with the emotion-generating amygdala, ensuring that we don't make our decisions with objective logic, despite our belief that we do.

So, people make hiring decisions emotionally; they only justify their decisions intellectually. The first step in qualifying the opportunity is to identify the hiring manager's needs. The most powerful needs in order are current pain, future pain, current opportunity, and future opportunity. Your job is to use research and open-ended questions to identify pain first, then opportunity.

A common consultant question is: "What keeps you up at night?" The goal is to identify the current pain of the client. You can modify that question and ask: "What problems are you actively working to address in the next three to six months?" By referring to the three- to six-month window, you focus the manager on the time it usually takes to fill open positions and potential early wins or successes you can achieve when you take the job.

Future pain is the next most powerful emotion. You can ask: "What issues or gaps, if not addressed, will cause problems for the organization in the near future?" Talk to any manager or supervisor about how they spend their time, and they will tell you it's usually fighting fires and dealing with customer problems. Everyone wishes they had more time anticipating and addressing issues before they become problems. Recognizing and addressing future pain is another way to achieve success at a new job.

Ask: "If you had a few more resources, what is the biggest opportunity available to you?" This question probes areas of current opportunity. It's often easier for employees from outside an industry to see and capitalize on opportunity. They don't filter their thinking with traditional assumptions, hamper their efforts by past failed attempts, or assume that something can't get done.

Ask: "What types of skills and experience will a leader need to be successful in the future?" This question gives you a window into the vision and strategy for the organization and the hiring manager's view on the talent needed to reach it. It allows you to differentiate between having a long-term future with the organization or filling a short-term need.

The next step in qualifying the opportunity is to market yourself as the best solution for addressing the hiring manager's needs. It is important to focus on their needs and not your wants. A traditional candidate with years of experience in the industry can openly talk about their requirements in terms of budget, staff, perks, development, etc. You must focus on how your skills, talents, and interests address pain first, then opportunity. Make the connections explicit and often during your interviews.

After completing my master's in business administration, I got a job with a healthcare organization. I had no experience in healthcare. I did not major in healthcare in college or graduate school, nor did I take healthcare courses. The early 1990s were a time of consolidation and acquisitions in the industry, with health insurers merging with other insurers and health systems vertically integrating by buying physician practices and expanding by buying specialty and ambulatory centers. I did know a lot about financing mergers and acquisitions and the problems associated with integrating companies. In my interviews with healthcare companies, I did not talk about my banking experience, knowledge of the media and entertainment industry, or financial skills. Instead, I positioned myself as the solution to the problem: "How do you finance, close, and integrate an acquisition?" I talked about the process that underlays all integrations, not stories about newspaper consolidation. I outlined the steps for creating a shared mission, vision, values, and strategic plan. In the end, I was able to persuade an organization to hire me that was about to buy a specialty center. I was able to progress within the company after it merged with another company.

The final step in qualifying the opportunity is to confirm that a decision will be made. This is an important step, but often overlooked. The decision people most often make is to do nothing. To give you the job, the hiring manager must be willing (decision), able (budget), and comfortable (sponsor) to make the decision. Your goal is to uncover the hiring manager's decision-making process. Who is involved? When will it happen? How will it happen?

I am not suggesting that you ask these questions directly but use indirect questioning to make sure that the opportunity is real. Consider the following questions:

1. **How long has the position been open?**
   If it has been open for a year, that might mean they have impossible standards or are unwilling to decide. If the role has been open for thirty to sixty days, it could mean the organization is ready to make a move or just looking to see what type of talent is available in the market.

2. **Is this a new position or an existing open position?**
   If it is an existing position, it implies that budget exists for the job. Follow up with: Who had this position before? Where are they now? If a new position, ask: What was the rationale for getting this job funded? What specific need does it fill? If it is a new role or department, it will require a greater internal network to get the department accepted within the larger organization. If you are transitioning from within the organization, ask yourself if you have the network and knowledge to promote the new department. If you are transitioning from outside the organization, quantify the support you will get to make the new area a success.

3. **Who, besides yourself, will you consult before making a hiring decision?**
   That question begins to uncover the decision process. You want to get a feel for where they are in the process—just starting, the screening phase, final-round phase, or offer phase. It also signals who has power and influence related to your role. It's a red flag if the hiring manager doesn't include others in the hiring process. It can mean that manager operates in a silo, therefore has limited influence across the organization.

4. **What types of references do you prefer?**
   This helps you understand the specific experiences, skills, and education the hiring manager needs to confirm before deciding to hire you. It tells an interviewer: You don't have to believe me, talk to others to confirm my story.

If you are lucky, after all that hard work you get the job! Congratulations. This is where most workers stop. But there is another part to the consultative sales approach—closing the deal.

Closing the Deal

Sales professionals are taught that there are two steps to close a deal: fulfillment and preventing buyer's remorse. These steps are particularly important when you are coming into a new industry, company, or role. You are an "outsider" with more to prove than a traditional candidate.

In general, fulfillment means the product or service delivers on the expectations the buyer had at the time of purchase. The hiring manager fulfills the employment contract by giving you the job, providing the tools and support, and removing barriers to success. You fulfill the employment contract by delivering results. Remember that giving you an opportunity is seen as a risk by others. The fastest and easiest way to remove that risk is to deliver results for your new manager. Work with your manager to get clarity around both your *what* (specific goals and objectives) and your *how* (the behaviors expected). Also, create a robust development plan that outlines the skills, knowledge, and experiences you need to thrive in your new role. You are playing catch-up compared to peers, so you can't afford to be lazy about development. The development plan helps identify opportunities to strengthen and enhance the skills you need for your current and future jobs.

The final piece of closing the deal is preventing "hiring remorse" by communicating results and building a robust professional network. Don't assume that your manager knows what you are doing. Communicate and get confirmation that you are delivering the expected results. Find ways for both you and your manager to communicate your successes to the broader organization. It is not about boosting or ego, but letting others get to know and like your work and building a reputation for accountability. Expanding your professional network signals to your manager that you are transitioning from "outsider" to "insider." You recognize the need to be accepted by others in your industry, and you are increasing your spheres of influence.

Case Study: Transitioning from Finance to Innovation Consulting

Henry Huang was on a successful finance career path. After graduating from the University of Connecticut with a degree in business administration, he joined Aetna's Internal Audit department. Over the next ten years, Henry got promoted, taking on roles with increasing scope and responsibility. He began his career as an audit consultant, moved to audit project manager, and then was promoted to audit supervisor. He went to school part-time to get his master's degree in accounting. He was a senior project manager for our e-business when we first met.

I was hiring staff to launch the new corporate university when he applied to be a program manager. Henry came across as confident though reserved during our interview, but he wanted to do something else. He was not quite sure what that something else was, but starting a new department sounded interesting to him. At this point he did not have the language to articulate what he wanted. After a couple rounds of interviews, Henry became part of the team.

Henry was responsible for creating the university finance and program infrastructure. He worked with me on vendor selection and management and produced the quarterly financial reports. He began attending our university programs in addition to completing his financial duties. Because we had a small team, I included everyone in off-site meetings where we created our strategy, reviewed the design of existing programs, and brainstormed new programs based on customer needs. These sessions immersed Henry in the language of strategic planning and thinking, instructional design, and customer-needs analysis. Over time Henry contributed more to the discussions, and the team discovered that Henry was creative. He frequently brought new ideas for programs and services and suggested ways we could make money offering tailored programs to business leaders. During our one-on-one meetings and development discussions, Henry was torn between becoming a certified financial analyst and shifting to a talent development career. He needed a safe way to test the new field, and that opportunity came when we started the General Manager, Profit & Loss Program.

The purpose of the GM P&L program was to identify and commercialize growth opportunities and prepare leaders to manage more complex businesses. The two-year program had four- to six-week mini courses in finance, sales/marketing, entrepreneurship/innovation, technology/operations, talent management, change management, and negotiation. This was the perfect opportunity for Henry. He used his financial background to help design and deliver the finance course while working with others to learn about the other areas. The GM

P&L program became Henry's "language lab," and he grew comfortable speaking the language of general managers. He learned that he had a strong interest in innovation and entrepreneurship. He was ready to make the transition from finance to consulting on innovation.

To progress, Henry needed formal training. He completed the Stanford University Innovation and Entrepreneurship certification program. This expanded his network and spheres of influence with people and organizations focused on growth through innovation. He attended the MIT/Harvard Medical School program on healthcare innovation. Henry's day-to-day job expanded to serving as a consultant to business units participating in innovation tournaments. Soon he began taking the lead on organizing and leading those tournaments. He worked with external consultants to create Business Immersion Experiences, one of our most popular programs.

Henry uses a line from Alan Kay, inventor of the graphical user interface: "Perspective is worth eighty IQ points." The most powerful way to change your perspective and discover new insights is to immerse yourself in another reality. Henry's Business Immersion Experience allows CVS Health leaders to share ideas and get a behind-the-scenes look at companies that are at the forefront of their industries.

We have taken leaders to Google, Apple, LinkedIn, PayPal, and IDEO, just to name a few. It is an opportunity for our leaders to expand their networks, build relationships, and discuss opportunities for collaboration. They examine how to adapt or adopt practices from other companies. Organizing these visits has expanded Henry's influence beyond CVS Health to other industries and other countries.

After getting formal training, expanding his network, and working with business leaders, Henry changed his image from a "finance" person to a "creative innovation expert." The transformation took five years and involved hard work. He was rewarded by being promoted to Director of Business Consulting Solutions for CVS Health. He works with business units to launch innovative ventures and pilot new products and services.

Case Study Insights

- **Look for win-win job assignments first**. The ability to offer value to an assignment or job based on your experience helps accelerate the transition and reduces hiring remorse. One of the keys to Henry's success was using his financial background to create the operational infrastructure of the new department. He contributed immediately by creating a course in an existing area of expertise.

- **Identify and pursue the right formal training based on work experience rather than exploration**. Education and training are most valuable when they can be applied to your current work. Too often I see colleagues pursue formal education in hopes that it will lead to the transition. Remember the employer's perspective? Education is usually at the bottom of the list. Find a way to get relevant experience first. Then use education to increase your probability of success on the job and to expand your network.

Case Study: Transitioning from an Ancillary Business to the Core Business Unit

Celia Peterson was successful in the investment industry. She created and ran a profitable department for Sanford C. Bernstein and Co. as manager of research services and then became the chief operating officer of Tower Capital, which provides capital to hedge funds, in New York City. Celia joined Aetna in 2004 to help the organization launch Aetna Capital Management, LLC, an asset management firm that managed a portfolio of hedge funds for Aetna, as well as outside investors' assets.

When I met Celia, she led all noninvestment-related functions of our asset management firm, including operations, marketing, and client services. She also served as the chief operating and chief compliance officer. When Celia sat in my office, she said she had a problem. The business unit she ran was closing. It was going to be an orderly wind down, so she had about a year to find another role in the company or leave to pursue outside opportunities. She had three school-age children and wanted to continue to work, but she was not sure what to do next. She had begun networking with others who suggested she speak with me.

I knew Celia had a lot of work to do. Despite her success, she was not part of the core business. Few people outside of the investment department knew what she, or her department, did. It was not even located in the corporate headquarters building but in a neighboring town. I started our session by asking her to identify her must-have and motivating factors. Celia identified intellectual stimulation, interdisciplinary opportunities, leadership, teamwork, and expert coworkers as her top five must-have factors. This meant Celia wanted to run a team of professionals working on diverse projects. She identified seeing things through, power, diversity of tasks, social justice, and challenge as her top five motivating factors. Her choices described wanting to have the power to address challenging issues to make a difference.

Next, we completed her job exploration summary sheet, and her selections surprised me. While she would entertain staying in the investment field, she was also open to the idea of exploring other industries, including the nonprofit world. She liked being a chief operating officer but would also consider public relations and chief of staff work. Going from investment banking to nonprofit is a big step. I suggested she needed to talk to a number of people. I shared the networking quadrant and asked her to reach out to others, then come back and discuss what she learned.

I was nervous for Celia after our first meeting. Networking would be key to her success. In my experience, clients find success networking, but it takes time. I always note the date when I meet with clients. The average length of time between my first meeting with a client and the second meeting is *two months*. That's right, I assign clients homework—either completing the Job Exploration Summary or speaking with those on their networking quadrant—and it takes sixty days for the average person to complete those tasks. I've found this to be true whether they are actively looking for a job or just exploring options while employed. That is why I was nervous for Celia.

Luckily, Celia was not the average person. She immediately spoke with many coworkers and would stop me in the hallway in the building to tell me about her conversations.

Shortly, she began to explore the possibility of finding a job with our corporate foundation. The foundation and its mission—"To promote wellness, health, and access to high-quality healthcare for everyone, while supporting the communities we serve"—hit all of her motivating factors.

After numerous conversations, although her interest remained, it became clear that the timing was not going to align for her to find an opportunity within the foundation. Celia, undeterred and now an expert networker, continued to speak to her network in the core business units. Celia soon found a corporate role that embodied the same motivating factors she was seeking in the foundation. As the Executive Director, Strategic Programs, she represented Aetna in an international initiative where global business leaders and investors collaborated to develop a mutually recognized framework to encourage and measure long-term value creation. She has since gone on to become vice president, strategy and business execution for CVS Health's Aetna Business Unit.

Case Study Insights

- **Always make a connection with the core business**. It is important to cultivate contacts and a relationship with the corporate headquarters and the business units that drive the revenue and profitability of the organization. This is particularly true if you are a remote worker. In the long run, your career opportunities will be limited by your network. Make the time to get to know employees across your major business units. Find ways to visit the corporate headquarters.
- **Be open to opportunities based on your motivating factors**. Use your must-have and motivating factors to evaluate your role fit. Understanding what she needed from a job and the things that truly satisfied her allowed Celia to pivot from working in the foundation to taking a job in the core business. On the surface, they looked like completely different jobs, but they both met her needs.
- **Start networking**. Celia was not afraid to network, but as I noted, clients will often wait two months to begin. Get started on your networking quadrant before you are forced to look for a job.

■ ■ ■

Making transitions from one industry or role to another is difficult but not impossible if you take a systematic approach. You need to learn new skills while showing industry insiders how your existing skills are transferable to the new area. You must take the time to build new relationships and networks to identify job opportunities. Finally, you must market yourself as the best solution to a problem experienced by the hiring manager.

As another example, Jen was a bright young entrepreneur who founded a social media company. Although she did not have healthcare industry experience, I hired her as my communications manager. It was a big transition. Now she was working in a large company with a more conservative culture. She handled the transitions beautifully. I had brought her in to create our department's social media presence. The problem was that there was a six-month delay in migrating to the new platform she was supposed to manage.

Jen had boundless energy, ambition, and a knack for solving problems. She used these transferable skills to support program leaders and simplify our operational processes. She read books, networked with experts, attended conferences, and took on extra projects to learn the language of her new industry. I promoted her once and she did the same thing, learning about talent development and how to grow leaders.

Next, she took a job as a human resources business partner to learn the advisory side of HR. After being promoted to senior HR business partner, she helped the new senior vice president of talent strategy with the integration of CVS Health after they acquired Aetna. During all of these transitions, the key to her success was the same: identify and address operational inefficiency. Jen hates wasting time and always finds ways to make processes, decision-making, and tasks more effective and efficient. This is her towering strength. She understands that learning the language of a new industry or department gives her the opportunity to use her towering strength in new ways.

Jen has come full circle and is starting her own company making online businesses more efficient and effective. She undertakes this business with greater knowledge of how larger organizations operate. Her company is off to a great start because she networked extensively to gain word-of-mouth business.

*Bottom line: Transitioning to a new industry
is like learning a new language.*

Making transitions is a special circumstance, but not the only type. People of color and women often face special development situations. In the next chapter, I will share my observations and particular considerations on this topic.

CHAPTER 9

Breaking Barriers: What Works for Women and People of Color

If we can learn to deal with our discomfort and just
relax into it, we'll have a better life.

—Mellody Hobson

The optimistic me dreams of a world where this chapter is viewed as outdated and irrelevant—a time when we live in a true meritocracy where all people's talents are recognized, valued, and used fully.

But the realistic me knows we are not there yet. It is necessary to acknowledge and address barriers women and people of color (also referred to as POC) face as they strive to develop and climb the corporate ladder. While this subject could be a book unto itself, I want to focus on ten areas of importance.

My observations come from a personal and professional perspective. As an African American leader, I have experienced firsthand over my thirty-plus-year career the struggles that affected me and my colleagues as we tried to develop and advance our careers.

Professionally, I have been a member of diversity and inclusion committees at two large organizations working to create and implement strategies to address inequity. I also facilitated diversity workshops and coached individuals as a consultant. Great progress has been made over time, and the understanding of and approach to diversity and inclusion has evolved. When I began my career, legal compliance and preventing lawsuits were the focus of diversity. Then it shifted to diversity as "the right thing to do." The next change I observed was creating the "business case" for diversity and why diversity improved the bottom line. The current focus of diversity is inclusion and creating an environment where all people can thrive at work. The focus of this chapter is strategies women and POC can use to address barriers.

Before I tackle the ten areas, I want to be clear about two concepts—awareness of the problem and the need to think differently.

Step one is awareness of why our general approach to solving inequity is not working. I will not spend time justifying a "call to action," saying we need to focus on diversity and inclusion because it is "the right thing to do," nor articulate the "business case" for diversity. Instead, please review the following statements:

- Women and people of color make less money than majority men for the same work.
- Women represent half the population but make up a fraction of the senior leadership roles in corporations.
- Compared to their percentage representation in the population and workforce, there are very few Fortune 500 companies led by women or people of color.
- There are few Fortune 500 boards of directors led by women or people of color.
- Across the globe, people of color are a faster-growing population segment than their white counterparts.

I encourage you to look on the internet and do your own research to see if you can refute any of the above statements. If you can, feel free to skip this chapter. If you can't, I ask that you read on with an open mind. Our current approaches are not working because of unconscious bias, a focus on the victim, and personalizing the issue.

I define unconscious bias as being unaware that our actions, beliefs, and judgments favor a person or group compared to another in an unfair way. I acknowledge that civil discourse on this topic is rare. I propose a compromise to move the conversation forward. Women and POC can stop labeling others as sexist and racists, which causes those people to become defensive, angry, and withdrawn. On the other side, majority people can acknowledge that even well-meaning individuals can act in a way that results in negative consequences for others. Further, we can accept that we judge ourselves based on our intentions, but others judge us based on impact and results.

If the five statements above are true, despite our best intentions and behavior, then our behavior must change. Simply being aware that unconscious bias exists and taking the time to question our assumptions will lead well-intentioned people to change their behavior in ways that support and benefit women and POC as they develop and advance through the company.

A focus on the victim is another significant barrier to progress. It is not women's or POC's fault that they've experienced inequality and barriers, but we love to focus on what they can do. This concept was best articulated by Anand Giridharadas in his book *Winners Take All: The Elite Charade of Changing the World*. In the book, Giridharadas quotes Adam Grant, an influential organizational psychologist:

> In the face of injustice, thinking about the perpetrator fuels anger and aggression . . . Shifting your attention to the victim makes you more empathetic, increasing the chances that you'll channel your anger in a constructive direction. Instead of trying to punish the people who caused harm, you'll be more likely to help the people who were harmed.[42]

While we all have a role in improving the situation, in general, women and POC don't have the opportunity to promote themselves; give themselves raises, bonuses, and equity; or appoint themselves onto boards of directors. Others who are part of the majority do that, so they are the primary engines of change. Focusing on what the victims can do may feel empowering, but it will not lead to the wide-scale change that we need.

Another barrier is the tendency to see problems as personal and individual rather than collective and systemic. As the head of talent management, I remember being in a meeting on executive talent succession and pointing out that although women were 76 percent of our total workforce at the time, they represented less than 25 percent of senior leaders. Stated another way, just because you are a man walking through the door, you were five times more likely to make it to the executive ranks compared to women. These statistics clearly described a systemic problem that needed an integrated corporate solution to resolve. Instead, executives asked to see the list of women I felt were passed over or were currently on an executive succession plan but not yet promoted to the next level. The next two hours were spent dissecting each individual and articulating reasons each person was not ready or qualified to become an executive. As a group, we refused to see the problem as systemic.

I've had similar experiences regarding people of color. As the head of talent development, I am often asked to share the number of POC in each of my programs. I am challenged to increase the percentage of POC across my high-potential programs. Sitting with someone in our workforce planning, diversity, and inclusion department one day, I asked two simple questions. First, how long have we focused on increasing the number of POC in special programs? The answer I got was a number of years. Second, how are we doing—have we significantly increased the percentage of POC getting promoted after graduating from our programs? The answer I got was no, the percentage has been consistent for a number of years. Given that, can we consider the possibility that the inability to achieve increases in the number of POC promotions is not because of lack of development? There must be systemic issues that need to be addressed.

Unconscious bias, focusing on the victim, and not recognizing systemic problems are erecting barriers for women and people of color. Addressing this is the first step to correcting inequity. Step two is acknowledging the need to think differently. There is a proverb that states "History is written by the victors." To use a new lens, I ask people to consider and then believe the following statement:

"If you don't see women and people of color, look closer because they are there."

When President John F. Kennedy addressed an estimated crowd of 40,000 in the Rice University football stadium on September 12, 1962, many people perceived that the United States was losing the space race to the Soviet Union. Russian cosmonaut Yuri Gagarin became the first man in space, ahead of the US Mercury project. At that speech, Kennedy said the famous lines, "We choose to go to the moon! We choose to go to the moon . . . We choose to go to the moon in this decade and do the other things, not because they are easy, but because they are hard, because that goal will serve to organize and measure the best of our energies and skills, because that challenge is one that we are willing to accept, one we are unwilling to postpone, and one we intend to win, and the others, too."[43]

The United States did get to the moon when Neil Armstrong was the first man to walk on the lunar surface as a crew member of Apollo 11 on July 20, 1969, fulfilling Kennedy's aspirational proclamation. Remember that saying that history is written by the victors? I grew up watching and hearing about the success of the Apollo program. And I never heard about any women or people of color in school or saw any in popular culture.

The Right Stuff was a 1983 film adaptation of Tom Wolfe's nonfiction novel chronicling the first fifteen years of America's space program. The film does not highlight any women at NASA. *Apollo 13* was a 1995 movie based on the events of the Apollo 13 lunar mission accident in which an oxygen tank exploded, and the heroic efforts taken to return the astronauts safely home. Again, no women featured. In 2016, thirty-three years after *The Right Stuff*, and one year after President Barack Obama presented the Presidential Medal of Freedom to Katherine Johnson, the movie *Hidden Figures* was released, highlighting African American mathematicians and aerospace engineers Johnson, Dorothy Vaughan, and Mary Jackson. Their work was instrumental to the success of the Apollo missions.

"If you don't see women and people of color, look closer because they are there."

Franklin Delano Roosevelt is considered by scholars to be one of the three greatest US presidents along with George Washington and Abraham Lincoln. He was the longest-serving president, from March 1933 to April 1945. FDR led the United States through the Great Depression and signed progressive legislation known as "The New Deal" that produced relief, recovery, and reform. He also guided America through World War II. Many schools discuss FDR, but few talk about Frances Perkins.

Frances Perkins was a Mount Holyoke– and Columbia University–trained sociologist who felt poverty was preventable. She became a

workers' rights advocate after the 1911 Triangle Shirtwaist Factory fire
in which 146 female workers jumped to their death because the building
lacked fire escapes. In 1929, then governor Franklin D. Roosevelt promoted Perkins to be the industrial commissioner of New York, the chief
post in the state labor department. When FDR was elected president,
he asked Perkins to join his cabinet. Perkins met with FDR and said she
would join his administration if she was allowed to push for her agenda.

Frances Perkins's February 1933 List for Franklin Delano Roosevelt

1. Forty-hour workweek
2. Minimum wage
3. Worker's compensation
4. Unemployment compensation
5. A federal law banning child labor
6. Direct federal aid for unemployment relief
7. Social security
8. A revitalized public employment service
9. Health insurance for all

I hung this list on my office door for a year. My point was twofold.
First, universal health insurance was the only thing on this list Frances
Perkins did not accomplish as US secretary of labor under FDR. At the
time I displayed the list, the House of Representatives and the Senate
were debating passage of the Affordable Care Act, the comprehensive
healthcare reform law enacted in March 2010. The list reminded people
that we have been trying to enact similar legislation for over seventy-
five years! When the law was passed, it provided access to healthcare,
expanded the Medicaid program, and promoted innovative medical
care delivery methods while reducing costs. Second, I challenged the
leaders I work with by asking, "What is on your list?"

With an understanding that long-term effective solutions to removing the barriers women and people of color face require awareness, a different lens, and systemic versus individual interventions by the majority
population, I want to turn now to what individuals can do.

The mindset I find most helpful when thinking about these issues is one I learned on a trip to the Disney Institute. We brought leaders there to go behind the scenes of an organization known for its unrelenting focus on delighting customers. During our visit, we learned about the Disney concept: "It might not be our fault, but it is our problem."

Imagine a family spending a full day at the park. They are excited but exhausted. They want to locate their car and drive back to their hotel, but they don't remember where they parked. Is this Disney's fault? Not really, but it becomes their problem if the last impression you have is frustration, hunting for your car after a long day.

Disney cast members are trained to help people find their car. Cast members write down the time when they begin to add a new row of cars in the parking lot. If they can determine an approximate time the guests arrived, they can tell in which rows to look for the car. Great service is about solving problems even if they are not your fault.

Since women and people of color are impacted by the actions of others, it is important to have strategies and tactics to manage around or through barriers others put in their way. Let's look at these barriers and how we can break them down.

1. Lack of Access to the "Engines" of the Organization

Many people are familiar with the term "glass ceiling"—an intangible barrier within an organization that prevents women or minorities from obtaining upper-level positions.

Although there are multiple factors that can contribute to the difficulty of upward mobility, one of the most common reasons is lack of experience with the most important functions or divisions of the organization. I call these areas the "engines." The exact areas depend on the organization but most often refer to the departments that generate the most revenue and profit. Women and POC are often disadvantaged by not getting leadership roles in these areas, instead leading peripheral departments and support functions. If you are looking for a senior or C-suite job, it is imperative to get exposure to your company's engines. If you are stuck, use the following questions to help identify your organization's engines:

- What are the top three revenue-generating departments, products, or services?
- What are the top three profit-generating departments, products, or services?
- What jobs have the largest spans of control (the greatest number of direct and indirect people reporting to them)?
- Looking at the backgrounds of the last three CEOs, presidents, or head of the job you aspire to, what leadership positions did they hold?

Armed with the answers to these questions, you can plot your career path. You can network to get jobs and exposure to those areas.

2. Others Making Assumptions/Decisions on Your Behalf

While affecting POC, I've noticed this barrier impacts women to a greater extent. Decision-makers feel entitled to speak on the behalf of employees when those staff members are not in the room.

The classic example: Bosses and team members deciding whether a woman should take on a new job assignment if they have children, or if they are thinking about having children. In the case of POC, people make assumptions about whether a client will feel "comfortable" working with someone who looks different than they do.

Greta was a learning and development consultant to Fortune 500 companies when I interviewed her to work on my team. It was a great fit. She was an expert in performance psychology with a doctorate in clinical and sports psychology. She had also worked for the army teaching resilience training. Greta quickly expanded the program offerings at Aetna University and developed a reputation for rapidly designing and launching programs business leaders wanted. I promoted her to lead our enterprise leadership development program. She also excelled in that role, winning praise from participants and senior leaders. I pushed Greta to interview for jobs outside of my area, as I did not have a role available that would stretch her abilities. She was eager for the challenge but was pregnant with her first child. I did not see this as a barrier and offered to speak with any hiring manager. I was surprised when two of Greta's friends and colleagues questioned my viewpoint. They asked me if I had considered her family and childcare situation. How was she going to handle the increased stress? One colleague said she would not come back to work after having her child. They concluded that she would be better off remaining a member of our team. Greta took the new role and is performing as I expected. She is respected by her new colleagues and continues to excel.

Tanya is an African American human resources executive with diverse industry experience. She is known for her calm demeanor, grace under fire, ability to work with the most difficult clients, and ability to build a strong team. She was tapped by senior executives to lead two integration teams after acquisitions. When identifying potential successors to our current chief human resources officer, Tanya was a clear front-runner in my eyes. Once again, I was surprised by the assumptions people made. One person said, "Tanya does not want to move back to Connecticut." Another person said, "Tanya does not want that position."

When asked if these comments were based on direct conversations with Tanya, both people said no. To their credit, they recognized their filters and agreed to speak with Tanya about the role.

In both examples, people's intentions may have been good but their impact can lead to missed opportunities and promotional setbacks. It is important for women and POC to clearly communicate their career expectations. Reinforce the desire to have people speak with you directly and not make assumptions about what you will or will not do. Invite people to consult you prior to making decisions or recommendations.

3. Promotions Based on Repeated Success Versus Potential

White men are typically promoted based on potential. If they perform well on the job, they are given opportunity with the expectation that they will excel in their next role. Women and POC are often promoted based on repeated success within a job. A typical promotion discussion sounds as follows:

"Brenden is doing a great job in Reno. He has exceeded his sales targets this past year and has built good relationships with clients. He has a lot of potential and is hungry. He reminds me of a younger version of me twenty years ago. The Nevada head of sales job is open; I think

Brenden is a good choice. It will be a stretch, but I believe he is up for the challenge."

Brenden gets the promotion and performs well. But the conversation about Tameeka, an African American woman, sounds different. "Tameeka has done a great job in Tulsa. She surprised me, exceeding her sales targets this past year and building good relationships with clients. The Oklahoma head of sales job is open, but I'd like to make sure Tameeka is ready for such a big job. Let's move Tameeka to Oklahoma City and see if she can be successful in a larger market. If she can, we'll find the right opportunity and promote her then."

Dr. David A. Thomas, president of Morehouse College, has done research on the career progression of minorities at US corporations. He found that whites and minorities follow distinct patterns of advancement. Specifically, promising white professionals tend to enter a fast track early in their careers, whereas high-potential minorities take off much later, typically after they have reached middle management. He also found that the people of color who advance the furthest all share one characteristic—a strong network of mentors and corporate sponsors who nurture their professional development.[44]

Brenden was promoted based on potential, while Tameeka must prove that her success was not a fluke. The impact is a slower career and wage progression for Tameeka. I don't think there is a lot you can do individually to combat this barrier. The key is to build networks of mentors and sponsors to intercede on your behalf.

4. Success Is Viewed as Individual, but Failure Is Collective

Many of my friends are particularly frustrated with this mindset. Success is viewed as individual. It sounds good on the surface to be viewed as an individual, but what is underneath is the mindset of exceptionalism. Your performance is not expected but outside of the norm.

Failure, on the other hand, is evidence of a collective deficiency. I've heard leaders say, "We tried a woman in that job and it did not work out." I started my career in banking and remember my first week on the job. After a couple of days, the person who sat in front of me turned around and said, "You know, there was a big discussion about where you should sit." When I asked why, he said, "Well, the last black person

that sat at that desk didn't make it through the program." I laugh now at that memory, but at the time I was dumbstruck. You really think the desk is the key to success?

Whether a woman, POC, or both, it is important to encourage people to see you as an individual and help them get comfortable with you as an individual. At the same time, it's helpful to remind people that failure is also usually individual and not collective.

5. Difficulty Getting Actionable Feedback and Sponsorship

One of the most difficult things for a POC leader to receive is good, actionable feedback and true sponsorship. A nagging question is: "Am I getting the same feedback and support as my majority colleagues?" Let's explore. The following is based on an actual review a POC leader received from his manager, Brian. I've changed the names and select details to keep the identities confidential:

> Lamont has had a very strong first half of the year.
>
> Lamont was the first to get his national account meetings set up, and he picked up three additional accounts this year (two smaller organizations and the one large account). For the remainder of the year, I would like to see Lamont continue to hold the firms and our internal partners accountable to enhance the relationships and drive outcomes from the meetings.
>
> Lamont and I have discussed next steps in his career, and I believe an excellent next step would be to lead a sales team or some other form of leadership position. Lamont is going to really ramp up his networking, and I encouraged him to let me know if he needs help getting time with specific individuals. It would be good for him to put together a list of key contacts for us to review and then discuss at future one-on-ones. For his part, I will also look to Lamont to continue to come up with training topics, so we can make sure he is fluent in all aspects of the business.
>
> Lamont has a strong future in the organization and clearly has a drive to continue to move forward with interesting challenges and is willing to move for the right opportunity.

So, what do you think? Is Lamont on his way to getting that next promotion? It was a very positive review. What is your guess as to when the promotion will occur? What follows is my response to Lamont:

First, congratulations on your review: it is obvious that your leader believes you are doing well, are proactive, and eager to get to the next level. But I assume you shared your review with me to go deeper. We can discuss action steps in detail in person or on the phone, but my preliminary observations are:

- Brian has done an excellent job focusing on what he expects from you including a) continue to hold firms and internal partners accountable; b) engage more with our largest national customers; and c) set up more meetings.
- Brian is currently a mentor or coach and not a sponsor (we can work on this), and all talk of improvement and promotion is put in your lap: a) "I am ready to assist . . . so let us know how we can help . . ."; b) "it would be good for him to put together a list of key contacts for us to review and then discuss"; and c) "I will look to Lamont to continue to come up with training topics so we can make sure he is fluent in all aspects of the business."

Lamont is doing well, but the promotion may be slower than he thinks. As noted, Brian is a mentor or coach and not a sponsor . . . yet. Mentors advise, guide, and offer support so you can achieve your career goals. Sponsors, on the other hand, advocate, connect you to opportunities, and help you build relationships so you can achieve your career goals. If Brian was a sponsor, he would tell Lamont the people he needs to know, highlight the best training he needs, and proactively connect Lamont with the right people.

So, what should Lamont do next?

We must analyze Lamont's relationship with Brian. If we assume Brian knows and likes Lamont's work (based on the review), then we must focus on getting Brian to know and like Lamont. People will sponsor you if they know and like you and know and like your work. To

move Brian into the sponsor camp, he has to establish more of a bond with Lamont. That means focusing on getting him comfortable with Lamont and his family. Dinner at his house, lunches, participation in areas or events of mutual interest. Getting to focus Brian on Lamont's image (30 percent) and exposure (60 percent) will lead to the promotion he seeks.

6. Being Killed with Kindness

My mother was an elementary school teacher, and this was the expression she used for well-meaning teachers who did not push their students to excellence: We are killing them with kindness. Imagine the English teacher who does not correct the grammar of the kids whose parents speak another language at home. See the math teacher who tells the minority student that getting a B on the test is great when they know with a little more effort they are capable of an A.

Kim Scott, cofounder and CEO of Candor, Inc. and author of *Radical Candor: Be a Kick-Ass Boss Without Losing Your Humanity*, describes it best in a business context. "There are two dimensions of good guidance: care personally and challenge directly. Most people want to avoid creating tension or discomfort at work. Bosses rarely intend to ruin an employee's chance of success or to handicap the entire team by letting poor performance slide. And yet, that is often the net result of Ruinous Empathy. Similarly, praise that's ruinously empathetic is not effective because its primary goal is to make the person feel better rather than to point out really great work and push for more of it."[45]

It is imperative to make people comfortable sharing their honest feedback. It does not mean that all feedback is valuable. Some you can discard, but I have seen more careers derailed by not getting good, honest, actionable feedback.

7. Not Being Plugged In to the Network of Power

Humans are social creatures, and it is important to plug in to the networks of people that have influence with the larger social structure. Unfortunately, life is like high school, and interacting with the "cool kids" increases your chances for success. Fortunately, people grow up and it is easier to be included if you add value to the group. If you are stuck, use the following questions to help identify your organization's networks:

- Which groups of people are usually right about promotions and changes in the organization?
- What departments or people have veto power over an idea or new product?
- Where do influential people socialize or meet outside of work?

Armed with the answers to these questions, you can identify strategies to connect with these people.

8. Image Is Even More Important

People notice how the boss dresses, what car they drive, and which leisure activities they engage in most. If you are a woman or POC, people pay special attention. Chapter 6 covers the importance of image and how to cultivate an image that propels your career. In this section, I will just highlight warning signs that your image needs attention. For women, these can include the following perceptions or phrases that are used as code for underlying beliefs or concerns:

- A hard worker who avoids office politics—you don't know or are unwilling to play the corporate game;
- Holds her tongue—people assume you don't know about a topic because you don't say anything;
- Consensus leader—you are a good team member or consultant, but you don't know how to make and substantiate your own decisions;
- Flirty—coworkers assume you didn't get ahead based on merit;
- Plays the gender card—people think you are angry and/or insecure and they might become uncomfortable with you;
- Conservative and not a risk taker—coworkers and managers believe you do not have the ability to grow an organization;
- Bitchy—you are not capable of balancing accountability and results with empathy and teamwork;

- Touchy-feely—you don't know how to drive for results or communicate using the language of business.

If any of the above images are attached to you, go back and read chapter 6.

For people of color, these can include the following perceptions or phrases that are used as code for underlying beliefs or concerns:

- Plays the race card—coworkers are uncomfortable with you and stop sharing information;
- Angry black person—other employees don't see you as approachable or someone they can trust;
- Diversity hire—people assume you were not hired based on merit;
- Nice person everybody likes—if everyone likes you, then you are not taking risks;
- Works hard—you may have to work twice as hard to be considered half as good, but no one ever got promoted purely because of hard work . . . this means they want to keep you in the position you are in and don't see you at the next level;
- Technical expert—people are limiting your career aspirations to one area;
- The super or good minority—people view Asians or Indians as compliant workers;
- Patient—if you exhibit too much patience, people will not see you as a leader.

If any of the above images are attached to you, go back and read chapter 6.

9. Negotiating Backfires

Francine Blau, a professor of industrial and labor relations and economics at Cornell University, has done a lot of research on the pay gap between men and women. She found three reasons that account for most of the estimated 20 percent gender pay gap: 1) job choice; 2) childcare or time away from work leading to less experience; and

3) negotiation and negative reactions to women negotiating. The remaining discrepancy can be attributed to bias.[46]

Mindset and skill are two keys to good negotiation. When it comes to mindset, I like what Mark Bertolini (former chairman and CEO of Aetna) used to say: "Make me say no." It is a simple phrase you can keep in your head to ensure you don't leave value on the table. Get comfortable with hearing the word "no." "No" does not mean people don't like you or think badly of you, or that they will rescind an offer—or at least, it shouldn't. Unfortunately, there are stories of women being penalized for negotiating a job offer. That doesn't mean you shouldn't try. If people get upset with you just for negotiating with them, trust me: you don't want to work for them in the long run. A willingness to engage in good negotiation shows professionalism.

Negotiation skill is the other key to addressing this barrier. In my programs I recommend *Getting to Yes: Negotiating Agreement Without Giving In* by Roger Fisher and William Ury, and *Getting Past No: Negotiating in Difficult Situations* by William Ury. At its core, good negotiation is about planning, knowing what you want, and getting others to understand the true value of what you offer an organization.

A Note to Sponsors

As I have stated before, the burden of removing barriers to success should not rest solely on women and people of color. So, this last point is for mentors and sponsors of women and POC, particularly male sponsors.

First, create a safe space that fosters interaction and builds trust. It is easier for men to meet with men, and women to meet with women, without people gossiping. It is important to create formal and informal settings for sponsors, mentors, and mentees to interact.

Second, proactively kill "relationship-related" rumors. It hurts both parties, so when appropriate, indicate that you meet regularly with high-potential employees both inside and outside of work. That usually stops the chatter.

Finally, help craft a shared vision of what is possible. A major disadvantage for women and POC is a lack of role models showing them what they can achieve. It is your job to help paint a vivid picture of the possibilities. Do not assume the people you are sponsoring will have any idea.

■　■　■

Assuming most people have positive intent and they are not trying to discriminate or hold others back, clearly communicating your aspirations, getting good feedback, and cultivating mentors and sponsors are the keys to success.

Kristin is a successful African American executive. When we met, she was chief of staff and the head of strategy for a specialty health product. At that time Kristin's ambition was to run a business on her own, to be responsible for a profit and loss center. In our one-on-one meetings, we talked about organizational strategy, image, networking, and gaining sponsors.

We analyzed the elements of the PIE model—performance, image, and exposure. I told her getting to the next level of executive is like joining an exclusive club: they have to let you in. During our conversations, Kristin would initially focus on performance, but I assured her she didn't need to do anything more in that area. The business she supported had exceeded all major metrics, and revenue had doubled in five years. Her strategies had been an important part of that growth. After three years, Kristin was named the executive director in charge of the profit and loss for her company, replacing the vice president who previously held the role. While she was frustrated not to be immediately promoted to vice president, I asked Kristin to focus on networking and gaining exposure to senior-level executives. As mentioned, people have to get to know you and like you to let you into the club. To her credit, Kristin did not become discouraged and continued to deliver superior results. On my end, I reached out to a number of people and asked them to consider her for vice president roles. After two years, Kristin was named vice president in charge of her own business unit. She is viewed as a strong P&L leader with a breadth of experience.

It might have taken longer for Kristin to get promoted when compared to her majority colleagues, but with persistence and focus on the right areas, image, and networking, she achieved her career goals. Kristin recognized she needed the help and support of others to succeed.

Bottom line: Don't be silent: ask for assistance and
demand people treat you as an individual.

I've covered the main areas of development: a) knowing what you want; b) understanding what employers want; c) networking effectively; d) understanding your leadership style; e) cultivating your image to get to the top; f) creating strategies for developing in your current role; g) making tough transitions from one industry to another; and h) navigating the waters if you are a woman or person of color.

Now it's time to pull it all together so you can take charge of your career.

CONCLUSION

Clear is kind. Unclear is unkind.

—*Brené Brown*

I believe the greatest untapped potential the world has is when people find and do the work they love. Organizations have a responsibility to develop competent, inspiring leaders who help staff members grow and develop. Individuals have the right to not just a paycheck, but to work at the intersection of their talents, abilities, and interests.

Develop is a road map to meaningful work. Working just to get a better title or bigger salary will not satisfy you in the long run. To feel truly fulfilled and contribute meaningfully to the world, you need to explore. *What types of people and culture work best for me? What types of problems do I like to solve? Who would benefit from my experience, knowledge, and skills?* You need a path to clarity. The goal of this book was to demystify and simplify how you can develop and grow in an existing role or make the transition to a new one.

Before you start using the tools to develop, you must come to understand what motivates you and makes you happy. Understanding your needs is important. I shared the list of work motivators (figure 1.1) to get you started, but use any tool that helps you better understand what aspects of a job matter most.

I ask people to start with recognizing the difference between "must-have" needs and what truly makes them happy. If you are looking for a new opportunity, culture fit should be at the top of your list. Culture represents the environment in which you will work, how things get done, how decisions are made, and how colleagues work with each other. If you can match your values and style with the culture of the organization, I believe your probability of success significantly increases.

Carl was a bright young manager working in human resources. He came from the defense industry and then transitioned to healthcare in conjunction with a family move. Carl pushed his team by raising standards, organizing their daily work, and showing his disappointment when his expectations were not met. In response, his team would challenge his authority, go behind his back to complain to Carl's boss, and not go the extra mile to complete work assignments. After an organizational redesign, Carl was taken out of his leadership role. It was at this point when he was referred to me for coaching and guidance. We had numerous conversations about the cultural differences between his old industry and healthcare and his lack of fit. Carl was smart enough, worked hard enough, and had the experience to be successful. He just was not advancing because he did not fit into a culture that was more indirect, collaborative, and relationship based.

After a good year of working with me, Carl decided to go back to his old company. They welcomed him with open arms, giving him a promotion, greater responsibility, and a team. We had lunch after his transition. He laughed as he informed me that coworkers on the new job told him to be more direct! Carl had not changed, but he was now in the right place.

Now it is up to you to take the next step. You can view the journey in four broad steps: a) sharpening your perspective; b) building and maintaining strong connections; c) creating a living development blueprint for success; and d) handling special situations.

Start with sharpening your understanding of what you want and what employers seek. Use the Job Exploration Summary tool to expand your options of what is possible. Listing your must-have and motivators (worksheet 1) can help you better define the culture that is right for you. The Constructive Questions tool lets you discover what experience, knowledge, and education is required to be successful in the job. Armed with this information, you can assess the fit between your interests and skills and the job's expectations.

Forging strong connections is the next step on your journey. The Mapping Your Experience tool shows you how to break down your experience and connect it to the roles you seek. Like an unpolished diamond, many clients I work with have the experience employers want, but they can't get others to see it. The tool shows you how to use more inclusive language to broaden your appeal. The Networking Quadrant tool helps you forge strong connections to identify new possibilities. It shows you how to turn the people who know you and know and like your work into a powerful team looking out for your best interests.

The Leadership Preferences Survey tool connects your leadership approach to the value you can add to an organization. Everyone can be a leader, but the tool helps you better define your leadership gifts and build a team that complements your style. Finally, the Spheres of Influence tool connects the image others have of you with your long-term goals. The image others hold of you must match your career expectations. Being an expert in your company is very different than being seen as an industry visionary. Influencing on a world stage requires different skills and background than being a regional or national leader. The tools help you navigate the transitions from subject-matter expert to industry thought leader to world leader.

The Development Plan tool serves as a living document and blueprint for growing on the job. It shows you how to align work experiences, learning opportunities, mentor and sponsor relationships, and your life experiences. Many clients only focus on work experiences, and by doing so, they limit their development. Coordinating work with other parts of your life produces a multiplier effect that accelerates your growth.

Addressing special situations was the last theme I covered. First, we looked at how to make the transition from one industry or role to another. In this case, learning a new language and communicating your transferable experience and knowledge are the keys to success. Then we explored the special situations women and people of color face navigating development. Getting actionable feedback, gaining the support of mentors, and finding the right experience are the keys to success.

Twenty-plus years of career development and counseling boiled down to seven tools. I hope you found a few nuggets of gold that you can use to achieve your career goals. Development, whether you are just starting out in your career or you are near retirement, is an important ingredient to happiness and job fulfillment. People who continue to develop on the job are more engaged and have higher levels of job satisfaction than those who do not.

Remember that life and our needs evolve over time. *Develop* isn't a one-and-done guide. You'll benefit from revisiting the tools again throughout the course of your career. At different stages of your career you will see greater value in some tools. For example, more experienced professionals often find greater value from the Spheres of Influence tool than early-in-career professionals. People who are just starting out or have worked in the same organization for a number of years love the Job Exploration Summary tool. So, I encourage you to pick up the book whenever you are thinking about your development.

Best of luck on your journey.

APPENDIX A

Leadership Preferences Survey

This tool will help you identify your preferred leadership style. There are no right or wrong answers. You can take the survey in this book and score it yourself. Or, visit tedfleming.com to take the test online and get immediate access to your scores.

Directions

Each item in this survey is made up of a statement followed by four possible endings. Indicate the order in which you believe each ending applies to you. Using the answer sheet, fill in the number in the box to the right of each ending and under the corresponding letter (A, B, C, or D). Fill in the number 4, 3, 2, or 1, indicating the degree to which an ending is most like you (4) or least like you (1). Do not use any number more than once for any group of four endings. Even if two or more endings seem equally like you, rank them anyway. Each statement must be ranked 4, 3, 2, or 1.

To have the most meaning to you, it is important that you respond as accurately as possible in terms of the way you believe you actually behave, not as you think you should behave.

Please review the following example. Once you are sure you understand the directions, complete the survey.

Example:

When working on a team, I tend to add the most value by:
   a. Developing new and different ideas.
   b. Adapting the creative ideas of others into products and services.
   c. Organizing the team members and their activities.
   d. Identifying the best people to be on the team.

Answer Sheet:

Question	A	B	C	D
1	2	1	4	3

Leadership Preferences Survey

Remember: 4 = most like you; 1 = least like you

1. **Given a work assignment, the first thing I want to know is:**
   a. The purpose and value of the assignment.
   b. How the assignment will benefit customers.
   c. The best way to get the project organized and under way.
   d. Whether I can complete the assignment alone, or if I will need help from others.

2. **When working on a team, I tend to add the most value by:**
   a. Developing new and different ideas.
   b. Adapting the creative ideas of others into products and services.
   c. Organizing the team members and their activities.
   d. Identifying the best people to be on the team.

3. **When I read about business in my leisure time, it is likely to be:**
   a. A research periodical or journal.
   b. An industry trade magazine, newsletter, or periodical.

   c. A popular business magazine like *Businessweek* or *Harvard Business Review*.

   d. A biography of an interesting person.

4. You are drawn to technology that:

   a. Changes the direction of your industry.

   b. Makes the customer/company interaction more effective.

   c. Makes the organization's operations more efficient and effective.

   d. Makes the people in the organization more effective.

5. When you think of people you like, you are attracted to:

   a. People who have interesting ideas and diverse interests.

   b. People who have friends from diverse backgrounds.

   c. People who are accomplished in their field.

   d. People who share your values and beliefs.

6. If you were in charge of turning around an organization, you would:

   a. Focus on developing new products and services.

   b. Focus on improving the service you provide current customers.

   c. Focus on improving operational efficiency and effectiveness.

   d. Focus on developing people and providing them with opportunities to shine.

7. When deciding to adopt a new idea, you are most persuaded by:

   a. Projections and models.

   b. Research and testimony.

   c. Real-life examples and analogies.

   d. Debate and discussion with other people.

8. To develop a person, the first thing you are most likely to do is:

   a. Create a development plan for the person.

   b. Identify courses that will increase the person's business knowledge.

   c. Identify job assignments that will build the person's skills.

   d. Identify potential mentors and coaches.

9. **You tend to measure the success of your organization by its:**
    a. Innovation performance (revenue from new products, market position).
    b. Customer performance (market share, customer satisfaction).
    c. Financial performance (revenue, ROI, cash flow).
    d. Employee performance (employee engagement, turnover, satisfaction).

10. **If your budget had $1 million in discretionary income to invest, you would:**
    a. Invest 50 percent in the R&D department and 50 percent in new technology.
    b. Invest 50 percent in market research and 50 percent in improving customer service.
    c. Invest 50 percent in new technology and put 50 percent in an emergency fund.
    d. Invest 50 percent in employee training and 50 percent in bonuses and other incentives.

11. **When I think about my organization, I:**
    a. Think about the future direction of the organization.
    b. Think about what I need to do today and a little about the future.
    c. Think about what worked in the past and how to apply it to the present.
    d. Think about what I need to do today to prepare for the future.

12. **People who know me would describe me as a good:**
    a. Strategist/innovator.
    b. Problem solver/relationship manager.
    c. Negotiator/team builder.
    d. Coach/mentor.

13. **When describing my weaknesses, people would say I am:**
    a. Not patient and/or not detail-oriented.
    b. Too willing to change and/or not focused on efficiency.

    c. Too detail-oriented and/or don't treat people as unique individuals.

    d. Too critical of people and/or take too long making decisions.

14. When analyzing the competition, I focus on their:

    a. Product and service offerings.

    b. Marketing and sales strategy.

    c. Business model and technology.

    d. People and corporate culture.

15. In a brainstorming or creative session, I usually:

    a. Come up with the most ideas.

    b. Calculate the value of the ideas.

    c. Explain the feasibility of implementing the ideas.

    d. Facilitate the process.

16. If I take a course or seminar outside of my field, I do so because:

    a. I'm curious to learn more about a specific subject.

    b. I want to extend my general knowledge.

    c. I'm interested in improving my professional knowledge.

    d. Someone I respect told me the course or seminar was useful for them.

17. I inspire people by focusing on the:

    a. Vision/strategy.

    b. Mission/market opportunity.

    c. Organizational goals/objectives.

    d. Values/contributions.

18. When negotiating or resolving conflict, I am best at:

    a. Getting all parties to focus on the problem.

    b. Understanding and articulating all parties' positions and underlying needs.

    c. Outlining mutually satisfactory options.

    d. Understanding and defusing the emotions of all parties.

19. **My communication skills are best used to:**
    a. Inspire people.
    b. Persuade people.
    c. Negotiate with people.
    d. Teach people.

20. **When managing a rapidly growing company, it is important to:**
    a. Keep the organization focused.
    b. Ensure that the organization does not neglect its core customer base.
    c. Develop the internal capability and capacity to handle the growth.
    d. Develop employee competencies to meet the increased demands on staff.

Leadership Preferences Survey

Answer Sheet

Question Number	A	B	C	D
1				
2				
3				
4				
5				
6				
7				
8				
9				
10				
11				
12				
13				
14				
15				
16				
17				
18				
19				
20				
Score:				
Total Score: A + B + C + D = 200				

After completing the survey, **total each column.** Then enter the column score below to get your results. For example: the total score in column A is your vision-centered leadership score.

Leadership Preferences Survey

Results

Your Leadership Preferences:	Score
Vision-Centered Leadership (Your "A" Total Score)	
Customer-Centered Leadership (Your "B" Total Score)	
Organization-Centered Leadership (Your "C" Total Score)	
People-Centered Leadership (Your "D" Total Score)	
Total Score (should equal 200):	

Interpreting Your Scores:	
65 or Greater	You **almost exclusively** use this leadership style.
60 to 64	You have a **strong preference** for using this leadership style.
55 to 59	You have a **moderate preference** for using this leadership style.
46 to 54	You **may** or **may not** use this leadership style depending upon the situation.
41 to 45	You have a **moderate disregard** for using this leadership style.
36 to 40	You have a **strong disregard** for using this leadership style.
35 or Less	You **virtually neglect** using this leadership style.

APPENDIX B

Quick Start Reference Guide

Use this guide to locate specific exercises and tools for your situation.

If you want to . . .	Use . . .	Go to Page . . .
Identify work values	Hygiene and Motivating Factors	6
Uncover job opportunities	Job Exploration Summary tool	14
Better communicate the type of job you want to other people	Job Aspiration statements	19
Understand how candidates are evaluated	Employer Interviewing Flowchart	26
Illuminate the employer's perspective	Constructive Questions tool	29
Prepare for a job interview	STAR Method exercise	40
Align your skills to a desired role	Mapping Your Experience tool	44
Start networking to forge strong connections	Networking Quadrants tool	54
	Your Networking Quadrants: Your Power Ten	63
Understand the leader's journey	Evolution of a Leader	74
Cultivate your image	The Three Ps of Image	109

If you want to . . .	Use . . .	Go to Page . . .
Expand your influence	Spheres of Influence tool	114
Develop in your current role	Development Plan tool	128
	FrameBreaking Model	129
Differentiate yourself from peers	Two Plus One Theory	139
Transition from one industry to another	Foreign Language lab approach	150
	Consultative Advisory Sales Approach	152
Learn success strategies for women and people of color	Nine Barriers Women and POC Face	173
Identify your leadership style	Appendix A: Leadership Preferences Survey tool	189

ACKNOWLEDGMENTS

Develop was a team effort, and I am grateful to all the people who helped me. Thank you to my wife, Kathryn Fleming, and Jennifer Grayeb for encouraging me to write and supporting me throughout the process.

The folks at BenBella were a joy to work with: my outstanding editor, Claire Schulz, who organized all my thoughts; Glenn Yeffeth, Lindsay Marshall, Monica Lowry, Sarah Avinger, Tanya Wardell, Adrienne Lang, Scott Calamar, Rachel Phares, and Aida Herrera.

Thank you to Jill Marsal, my agent, who patiently answered all of my questions, and Margaret Greenberg for introducing us and supporting me.

Special thanks to my team and Christine Valluzzi, Henry Huang, and Chris Leet, who were there from the beginning. Finally, I want to thank everyone who allowed me the privilege of guiding their careers. Their willingness to share personal stories and try my ideas has made me a better consultant, coach, and business advisor.

NOTES

1 Frederick Herzberg, "One More Time: How Do You Motivate Employees?" *Harvard Business Review* (February 2003): 87–96.

2 Herzberg, "One More Time."

3 Kimberley A. McGrath and Bridget E. Travers, eds., *World of Invention: History's Most Significant Inventions and the People Behind Them* (Detroit: Gale, 2001).

4 Simon Sinek, "Start with Why: How Great Leaders Inspire Action" TEDxPugetSound, September 28, 2009, www.youtube.com /watch?v=u4ZoJKF_VuA.

5 Robin Dunbar, *How Many Friends Does One Person Need? Dunbar's Number and Other Evolutionary Quirks* (London: Faber and Faber Limited, 2010).

6 Kevan Hall, *Making the Matrix Work: How Matrix Managers Engage People and Cut Through Complexity* (Boston: Nicholas Brealey Publishing, 2013).

7 Hall, *Making the Matrix Work.*

8 Hall, *Making the Matrix Work.*

9 Will Kenton, "Triple Bottom Line" Investopedia, last modified January 31, 2020, www.investopedia.com/terms/t/triple-bottom-line.asp.

10 Eddie Griffin, "Excerpt from You can tell 'em I said it!" YouTube, September 18, 2012, www.youtube.com/watch?v=tvpS21VbGHY.

11 Charles Jacobs, "Narratives That Transform the World" TEDxBeaconStreet, December 7, 2017, www.youtube.com /watch?v=y6VWm9wm0h4.

12 Junji Noguchi, "The Legacy of W. Edwards Deming," *Quality Progress* 28, no. 12 (December 1995): 35–38.

13 W. Edwards Deming, "14 Points" Wikipedia, en.wikipedia.org /wiki/W._Edwards_Deming.

14 John Wooden, "John Wooden Coach & Teacher," Official Site of Coach Wooden, www.coachwooden.com/.

15 Wooden, "John Wooden Coach & Teacher."

16 Isabel Briggs Myers, *Introduction to Type: A Guide to Understanding Your Results on the Myers-Briggs Type Indicator,* Sixth Edition (Palo Alto: CPP Press, Inc., 1998).

17 Jason Hedge, *The Essential DISC Training Workbook: Companion to the DISC Profile Assessment Volume 1* (Redding: DISC-U.org, 2013).

18 Angela Duckworth, *Grit: The Power of Passion and Perseverance* (New York: Scribner, 2016).

19 Harvey J. Coleman, *Empowering Yourself: The Organizational Game Revealed,* Second Edition (Dubuque: Kendall/Hunt Publishing Company, 2005).

20 Peter Cappelli and Anna Tavis, "The Performance Management Revolution," *Harvard Business Review* (October 2016): 58–67.

21 Sylvia Ann Hewlett, *Executive Presence: The Missing Link Between Merit and Success* (New York: HarperCollins Publishers, 2014).

22 Gregg Lichtenstein, PhD, "Fostering Entrepreneurship," interview by Ted Fleming, June 2018.

23 "Mother Teresa Biography," Biography.com, last modified February 24, 2020, https://www.biography.com/people/mother-teresa-9504160.

24 David Rock and Heidi Grant, "Why Diverse Teams are Smarter," *Harvard Business Review* (November 4, 2016).

25 Al Ries and Laura Ries, *The 22 Immutable Laws of Branding: How to Build a Product or Service into a World-Class Brand* (New York: Harper Business, 2002).

26 Ries and Ries, *The 22 Immutable Laws of Branding.*

27 Malcolm Gladwell, *Outliers: The Story of Success* (New York: Little, Brown and Company, 2008).

28 "Oprah Winfrey Biography," Biography.com, last modified January 22, 2020, https://www.biography.com/media-figure/oprah-winfrey.

29 Mark Kizilos, "Intensity and Stretch: The Drivers of On-the-Job Development," *Experience-Driven Leader Development: Models, Tools, Best Practices, and Advice for On-the-Job Development* (San Francisco: John Wiley & Sons, Inc., 2014).

30 Kizilos, "Intensity and Stretch."

31 Cynthia McCauley, "Identifying Development-in-Place Opportunities," *Experience-Driven Leader Development: Models, Tools, Best Practices, and Advice for On-the-Job Development* (San Francisco: John Wiley & Sons, Inc., 2014).

32 Timothy D. Wilson, et al., "Just Think: The Challenges of the Disengaged Mind," *Science* 345 no. 6192 (July 2014): 75–77.

33 Amos Tversky and Daniel Kahneman, "The Framing of Decisions and the Psychology of Choice," *Science* (January 30, 1981).

34 Anders Ericsson and Robert Pool, *Peak: Secrets from the New Science of Expertise* (New York: Houghton Mifflin Harcourt, 2016).

35 Ericsson and Pool, *Peak: Secrets from the New Science of Expertise.*

36 Ericsson and Pool, *Peak: Secrets from the New Science of Expertise.*

37 Sandra F. Witelson, Debra L. Kigar, and Thomas Harvey, "The Exceptional Brain of Albert Einstein," *The Lancet* 353 (1999): 2149–53.

38 Daniel Goleman, *Emotional Intelligence: Why It Can Matter More Than IQ* (New York: Bantam Books, 1995).

39 Charles Stansfield and Jeanne Hornor, "The Dartmouth/Rassias Model of Teaching Foreign Languages," US Department of Health, Education & Welfare National Institute of Education (1980).

40 "Study Abroad and Off-Campus," Dartmouth College, accessed March 3, 2020, https://home.dartmouth.edu/education/undergraduate-experience/study-abroad-and-campus.

41 Charles S. Jacobs, *Management Rewired: Why Feedback Doesn't Work and Other Surprising Lessons from the Latest Brain Science* (New York: Penguin Group, 2010).

42 Anand Giridharadas, *Winners Take All: The Elite Charade of Changing the World* (New York: Alfred A. Knopf, 2018).

43 John F. Kennedy, "Moon Speech—Rice Stadium," September 12, 1962, NASA, accessed March 3, 2020, https://er.jsc.nasa.gov/seh/ricetalk.htm.

44 David A. Thomas, "Race Matters," *Harvard Business Review* (April 2001).

45 Kim Scott, *Radical Candor: Be a Kick-Ass Boss Without Losing Your Humanity* (New York: St. Martin's Press, 2017).

46 Francine Blau, "Mind the Pay Gap," interview by Stacey Vanek Smith and Cardiff Garcia, National Public Radio, April 9, 2018.

ABOUT THE AUTHOR

Ted Fleming is passionate about helping people reach their full potential. He has more than thirty years of experience in the healthcare, financial services, and education industries as a strategic planner, consultant, business owner, and general manager. He is currently head of talent development for CVS Health. Ted graduated from Dartmouth College with a degree in economics, and the Fuqua School of Business at Duke University with a master's in business administration. Ted is an avid tennis and squash player. He lives in Connecticut with his wife, Kathy.